Good Practice Guide

Business Resilience

Mark Kemp

RIBA Publishing

RIBA Publishing, 2022

Published by RIBA Publishing, 66 Portland Place, London, W1B 1AD

ISBN 978 1 91412 407 5

British Library Cataloguing-in-Publication Data
A catalogue record for this book is available from the British Library.

Commissioning Editor: Alex White
Assistant Editor: Clare Holloway
Production: Richard Blackburn
Cover design by Design by S-T Ltd
Designed by Studio Kalinka
Typeset by Academic + Technical, Bristol
Printed and bound by Page Bros, Norwich

Image credits
Figures 2.1, 2.2 Mark Kemp

www.ribapublishing.com

FSC www.fsc.org MIX Paper from responsible sources FSC® C023114

Contents

Acknowledgments

If Helen Castle had not asked me to write this book it wouldn't exist. I didn't know I had it in me. That I have been able to say anything at all about business is down to Bob Platts, who taught me how to take over his practice. Without Alex White's patience and elastic deadlines, I'm not sure it would ever have been finished. Readers should be particularly grateful for Neil Gallacher's punchy edits on early manuscripts, which reduced some abominably long sentences, and Alasdair Deas has been invaluable in scouring the final copy for edits to really bring out the meaning. Individual contributions by Paula Wilmore and Gavin Sorby offer progressive examples of how to stretch practice. Their assistance with case studies, along with the help of Martin Back, Rob Woolston, Tara Gbolade and Dhiran Vagdia, has provided generous, real-world context for comparison. Time given freely by professional colleagues and clients, including Andrew Baker, Nicky Francis, Ian Whittock, Diana Heal, Jason Clark, Marsha Ramroop and Martin Sheldrake, helped ensure non-architecture subjects were checked by non-architects. My thanks to these people, and to my family Deb, Esme, Molly and Christian for their tolerance of my absenteeism and for providing constant, unwavering support through long nights until it was finished.

About the author

Mark Kemp has been the sole director of PLACE architects Ltd since 2009 and has been involved in construction for over 30 years. After working on site in London and attending night school in Hammersmith, he went on to study architecture at South Bank University and graduated in Plymouth.

He was on the board of RIBA Enterprises for three years, overseeing the partial equity sale of that business, and held the offices of vice chair of the Board and chair of RIBA Enterprises' Risk and Audit Committee. He was on the Finance and Operations Committee for the RIBA for five years to 2020 and now chairs the *RIBA Journal* Editorial Panel.

It is the engagement with so many people that has always been his passion – especially when there is a knotty problem to unravel. When he is not working, he can be found cooking for his family in Exeter, listening to football commentary on 5 Live.

Introduction

To survive in business, you need to make money and be resilient. But everything changes, and events – both planned and unplanned – will test your business continuously. A resilient business will bounce back after it's been bent all out of shape by difficult or unexpected circumstances. To be resilient requires agility, adaptability, strength and resources.

So, how do you make a business that has all those things?

Systems and structures will help keep a business afloat, because they monitor important matters, such as time and cash flow, but only people can make decisions. Being in charge of a business requires a response to challenges at every level, whether financial, operational or reputational.

Running a business requires you to do the following:

- **Listen** – if you hear even the slightest sound of anything requiring attention, act straight away and do something. Do not wait.
- **Communicate** – constantly tell people what you need them to know, whether they are staff, clients, builders or co-professionals. You will have to repeat yourself.
- **Thank everyone** – aim to say 'thank you' a minimum of seven times in seven different ways for every one thing someone does for you. It's easier to do than you think.
- **Be selfless** – put the needs of others before your own, and never complain about what you have to do, but be crystal clear about what you expect of them.
- **Be humble** – don't be too proud to say sorry, even on behalf of others, while remaining blisteringly honest. Always ask for help.
- **Never assume** – know what you don't know. Examine each situation forensically to ascertain the facts of the matter. Ensure you ask the critical questions to get on top of precisely what you need to plan a course of action promptly.

In 2006 I became the co-director of an architects' practice. At the end of 2009 I bought the company and have been the sole director ever since. I borrowed money to buy the practice, and spent the next three years paying off the loan. For too long after the 2008 financial crisis, I used to say my business plan was to remain a going concern. I was only half-joking. By 2013, I was in charge and free of debt, but all I was doing was running the practice I had taken over. I had not really thought about where it would go or what I wanted it to become.

I was fortunate to take over an established business with a reputation, which meant we had referrals and repeat business. In short, it was a going concern; my business plan objectives were being met. There were good office procedures already in place and all I needed to do was keep them running. There was a sound resource planning method too, which, although time consuming, would provide warnings when work was falling short.

I knew I wanted to grow the business and tried several different approaches to achieve this. I collaborated with a larger local practice to build a platform to access larger, more varied projects – it didn't work. I entered a competition with a contractor and a manufacturer to provide self-build units by creating a unique offer – we didn't win. I agreed to subcontract our services to provide white label RIBA Stage 4 drawing packages (technical drawings issued with no title block, allowing the recipient to check and issue them as part of their data drop) to a much larger practice based in the Midlands which was busy – but this didn't happen either.[1]

The reason none of these attempts came to anything was because I didn't have a clear idea of where the firm was going – consequently, I was never going to get there. It's like making a planning application without a design proposal; I simply didn't have a plan. To be successful, you must set out your vision and describe how you will get there. If you don't tell people who you are, what you do and what you want, nobody is going to know.

When you start the process of examining what defines your practice, it is critical to include your staff. Start by asking them what they think the practice is – they may know better than you. If you include them, and you work out together what they can offer and where they fit in the plan, it is more likely they will be behind you in trying to implement any changes to the way you run the business. Working out a shared vision is a lot easier than doing it on your own, but even then it can take a considerable time to figure it out.

You may need to review a body of completed work in terms of scale, sector, clients and style. Not all of it will support what you might initially think is going to be your vision and you must be pretty ruthless, admitting when it isn't what you expected it to be. For new practices the exercise will be different – and in some ways a little easier, because there isn't an existing portfolio – but you must still plan what you want and agree this with the people you work with.

You need to be unswerving without being rigid, clear minded without being fixed, and sturdy while remaining agile.

It is vital that you know your business in detail. You must record time and activities, and use those records to provide you with achingly transparent data showing where you have gone wrong and what you can do differently next time. You must know the costs of everything unproductive – not just the things that make you money. You need to calculate how much time you waste and what the residual amount is worth to you. All this on its own won't make a resilient business, but it will help you make a judgement call when you need to.

Your decisions count. You have to be patient and analyse what is in front of you. How you respond to unexpected situations is the difference between having a resilient business and one that is fragile. This guide suggests ways to help you shape the context you work in and invest in the people around you to create an environment and a culture of resilience – making you more likely to survive in business.

Endnote

1 In fact, it did in the end, but not until several years later.

Part 1

Organisations

1

Practice

Businesses are organic, and if organic things do not grow, they die. Your business – and architects' practices are businesses – needs to grow like every other business, which means taking a bigger share of the market you trade in, attracting new projects and building in resilience as a way to mitigate risks. If you lead a business, the mindset to grow must start with you. Growth is not simply about getting bigger, it can be about developing skills, reputation or inclusivity. All of these represent valid growth propositions; growth is about moving and not staying still. The vision for the business will be shaped around this ambition.

Mapping out a plan over a three- or five-year period will help you to sustain your business vision. You should include your staff in this process, and embrace their key strengths in the plan. This will get them on board, so they are committed to the plan and willing to work with you to achieve it. Reviewing the plan together at regular intervals introduces accountability and challenge, but combats fatigue and stagnation; it will create a culture of learning and improvement, which benefits both the staff and the business.

Every decision taken should be aligned to the objectives of the business; from what equipment should be in the office and how software can be enhanced or augmented, through to how much should be invested in training and how to allocate tasks among staff. To introduce improvements, you first need to build up a detailed picture of how your business operates and where it might fall short. Assessing staff and the value they can offer a practice is one alternative to the standard approach of using recruitment to meet a need. By considering the culture and nature of your practice, it is possible to rethink the distribution of activities and how efficiencies can be gained.

Plan your goals and break down the activities of your business so you can stay on track and head towards what you want to achieve. In the same way that a design project evolves from a brief to a set of construction drawings, developing only the relevant level of detail as it rests on each one of the stages, these methods progress from general aspirations to specific actions. This means you can adjust your business plans when needed (or forced) without losing sight of the 'project brief', which in this case is the vision for the business.

The following sections are a starting point for building structural resilience into your practice by thinking about the business direction and set-up.

Direction

In order to have a resilient business, you must be able to make decisions that will lead to actions that help the business maintain profitability. To inform this decision-making, you need to have four key documents: vision, mission, business plan and strategic plan. In themselves they can't do anything, they are just tools for use, but they should help provide a clarity not possible without them. Even the process of writing them will tell you more about what you want to achieve and what you don't, more so than if you just talked about them. These documents are summarised in Table 1.1.

Your vision, mission and business plan will each have a different service life.

The *vision* is the intended future for your business. It is expected your vision will be long-lasting because it reflects who you are and what you want to be recognised for as a business; it would not benefit from being revised every week.

Table 1.1: Definitions of key documents

Document	Definition
Vision	A concise outline of what your practice aims to achieve or become in the future. It provides direction and purpose for the business and its staff.
Mission	A concise outline of what your practice does now and how it is different to other practices. It defines why you exist and what you deliver.
Business plan	A description of how your practice creates, captures and delivers value. It sets out your objectives and goals to help others support you.
Strategic plan	A list of actions or tasks, and how they are to be implemented, that will lead to your practice succeeding in reaching its vision.

The *mission* is a snapshot of what the business tries to do to achieve your vision – almost like describing what you do on a journey you are taking to reach a destination. The activities you perform along the way are not likely to vary much unless you change the nature of your business. However, the path itself can be varied and changed, provided it ultimately leads to your vision.

The *business plan* is like the route map to the vision and is usually restricted to one year, three years or five years. It charts your preferred course to reach your destination, but it can also change. In fact, it has to be able to change, because this part is affected by real world events. Your business plan must be flexible enough to withstand being blown off course temporarily, before you have a chance to navigate back to where you need to be – which is heading towards your vision.

> Those able to understand and react to the evolving situation quickly and appropriately will not only survive but will also create a more resilient organization.
>
> Frank Gerhard, Marie-Paule Laurent, Kyriakos Spyrounakos and Eckart Windhagen[1]

If you were to imagine these managerial devices in financial terms, the vision can be seen as the amount you want to make, the mission is like your annual accounts, with an end of year report explaining what your business is, and the business plan can be seen as your initial proposals, stating which financial instruments you need to invest in to reach the desired amount and set out a bit like your budget. Underpinning these will be your practice's day-to-day management accounts, or 'books', containing cash flow forecasts, profit and loss calculations and various reconciliations, as well as targets for your staff to achieve. These relate to your everyday activities – in running a business, these management accounts may be seen as the equivalent of a strategic plan.

The *strategic plan* will list a set of strategic objectives, each requiring a task to be performed by someone within a time frame and to a budget. The completion of each task will bring the business closer to its vision. The strategic plan is the most fluid of the management planning tools and provides the levers to accommodate the changes you will experience, whether planned or (more likely) unplanned, to bring the company direction back on track. The frequency with which these tasks will change is a function of the business environment you are operating in at the time.

A strategic plan can incorporate all manner of aspects within your business, as well as those external to it – from the core function of the business to promotions through advertising, building staff capacity, or aiming to increase turnover through targeting new business in specific areas. It is a planning tool that also provides you with a way to be flexible when things are not going according to plan. It is a space where key decision-making can take place rapidly, such as when a new course needs to be set in response to a setback such as a lost revenue stream. At the same time, it allows you to keep an eye on the reasons for making changes without losing sight of their purpose, which is to meet the strategic objectives.

There could be situations that require a fast, decisive response and even a change of direction for the practice. Provided such changes align with the practice's vision, the staff, and hopefully clients too, will understand the reasons for it and will then have confidence in the changes. Changes in business can be unsettling to staff, making them feel nervous about their position or their future. Preferably, decision-making about such changes should involve staff members, securing their agreement to adjust without delay the way they have been doing something.

Maintaining business continuity and ensuring resilience to factors that threaten trading requires maximum adaptability and full buy-in from staff members. Keeping staff on board, all pedalling in the same direction, is the best way to ride out whatever difficulties you might be experiencing.

PRACTICE INSIGHTS

Strategy

In 2015, I became a non-executive director on the board of RIBA Enterprises (a subsidiary of the RIBA), a sales-driven knowledge base responsible for producing the National Building Specification (NBS) and which employed nearly 250 staff. In the boardroom, we were presented with reports from the executive on all matters relating to running the business and it was soon apparent that the effort they directed towards their staff was considerable. They held an annual 'strategy day', with speakers, questions, workshops and presentations about the future direction of the business. On the train home, I thought: Why haven't I ever held a strategy day? I only had nine members of staff, what could possibly go wrong?

The afternoon in December 2016 when we held our first strategy day – in a small, rented conference room – was a turning point. The facilitator, David Crawford, who was a marketing expert, had interviewed staff individually before the event and learned something about each of them, including their role and the part they played in the practice. By the end of the day, we had agreed three things:

- We needed another member of staff.
- We needed better CAD software.
- We needed new offices.

By June 2019, we had achieved all of them, and more.

We were only able to meet these aims because we set them as goals. They emerged from a free discussion in which people spoke about what they enjoyed and did not enjoy about their work, what they wanted from it and where they wanted it to take them. Other things emerged, such as a lack of understanding about what other members of staff did – particularly between administration staff and drawing office staff. This was initially surprising, given the small number of staff, but it highlighted that effort was required to resolve the issue. People work together at their best when they understand each other's role.

Even after a successful strategy day, the hardest thing was to agree a vision and a mission for the future direction of the practice. Around 18 months on from that day, on behalf of a client I asked the local council how they would support a new business to develop a new visitor attraction. The council suggested that the Growth and Skills Hub might be able to help with tourism marketing. In setting up the contact, the opportunities the Growth and Skills Hub were offering to provide for my client struck a chord with me, so I rang them back to ask if it would be inappropriate to ask if they could also help me. They said they could – and they did.

The assistance was available through the European Structural and Investment Fund. In addition to analysis of our emerging digital requirements and possibilities for staff training, the Hub also provided 15 hours of executive coaching. After one session with Matthew Porter from Oxford Innovation, it was clear the critical missing pieces of the business were the vision and the mission – without these, nothing else had anything to connect back to. Before the next session I set up a subcommittee of staff members for the remaining hours and, using a technique called a Vision Orbit, we finally formed our shared vision.

Having a vision and a mission was immediately unifying. It focused everyone's mind on who we said we were – it meant we could now focus on being what we said we wanted to be. It made decision-making easier because we now had reference points we could refer back to – when something needed to be decided we would consider whether it represented our image of ourselves. It also meant we could explain who we were in a consistent way, whether to other people, each other or new members of staff.

Induction programmes are the perfect vehicle for introducing the firm's goals and ambitions to new staff, but this messaging should not be reserved just for new starters. Including everyone empowers members of staff to become ambassadors for the firm when they are out and about – it can and should even engender a sense of pride. It particularly helps to take the focus off the person. It is not always so easy to sell yourself, especially for small practices or sole traders, but to present a business vision depersonalises the process in a good way – it can remove the need to self-doubt or self-deprecate and affords the chance simply to be honest about the service your practice offers. And 'selling' is key – although still sometimes seen as vulgar, it is critical to establish selling as a core part of the practice.

Capital

You are in business to make money through providing your services. If your overheads are low and steady, and you are certain of a regular stream of work, you will probably be able to sustain your business without having to borrow money or seek additional investments. However, your income will probably be insufficient to allow you to grow the business. Whatever you may feel about growth, it is essential – so don't quibble about it, aim for it. You can have discussions about the nature and rate of growth, and the scale of business you are going to aim for, but you can't get on by saying you don't want to grow.

A resilient business has to make a profit. The larger the scale of the business, the lower the proportion of fixed costs, which should improve the stability of the business, making it more profitable.

Capital investment

Parts of your business plan will require funding; activities such as marketing and investments in technology, staff and training all require a budget. This is known as *capital investment*.

You can either self-finance from within the business or borrow from a third party. If it is your own money, you can choose simply to give it to the business as a loan from yourself (it is important to appreciate the business has a separate legal identity to you so payments made into the business must be properly accounted for). You could raise funds from within the business to reinvest in the practice, increasing your working capital (see below).

If the money is coming from a third party, they will want the sum borrowed to be returned with interest and within a certain timescale. Some architects take the view that running a business is enough of a risk without adding borrowing into the mix. They might be right, although this depends on the individual's risk tolerance and the credibility of the business proposition. You will have to ask yourself whether the investment will return material additional profit above the cost of the finance over the term of the arrangement.

Once you have chosen what you want to improve, first set down the amount of money you will need and when. For instance, if you plan to spend on marketing, agree how long you want to run a campaign for, what you want to achieve from it and how will it affect your profits. The impact on profits is the ultimate measure of effectiveness, called the 'return on investment' (ROI), and it is the bit most people want to know. You could take a long-term view and accept that you will not increase profits in the short term; for instance, investing in marketing will increase your exposure and get your name known, leading to a steady increase in business over a longer period of time. Or you might choose to invest in new software first – but the process is the same. Work out how much money you need by considering the cost of the new equipment, the cost of the training, the estimated cost of downtime (as you or your staff learn new skills and perform tasks more slowly initially), then apply a timescale to this and assess what the benefits are – the ROI.

Above all, ask yourself 'Is this worth doing?' This is a judgement call, but check it against your vision – does it take you in the right direction? The investment plan is a forecast and will invariably be at odds with the actual outcome. However, as long as the assumptions are objective and well researched, it should provide you with sufficient information to make an informed investment decision. When you have a number, a timescale and a sound reason for making the investment, write them down as your business case for borrowing.

Working capital

At the same time you are investing in growth, you need to maintain an amount of money in the bank with which to keep the business going. This is known as your *working capital*. The amount of working capital you need is based on an assessment of your current assets against your current liabilities (see *Financial Management* by Brian Pinder-Ayres[2]). Put another way, it is the amount of money you need to keep in hand over a certain period to ensure you can pay your dues (staff costs, bills etc.).

The amount of working capital you need is a function of the time it takes to get money owed to you into your bank account. If it takes you a long time to collect money from your clients, the amount of working capital you need to have available (to prevent you running low on cash) will be higher than if you can get the money in more quickly – result: a high level of working capital.

You can reduce your working capital requirement quite simply by billing more frequently and charging more for your time. You might not be able to get clients to pay a new, higher rate straight away, but you should see that, if you do this, you will increase the money coming in (asset), and if you can get clients to pay more quickly, you can reduce your working capital even more. If you can achieve this, you will have more money available to reinvest in your growth plans.

Reducing your working capital can be a good way to increase the amount of money available within your business for capital investment. You might choose to do this if you were going to adopt 'building capacity within the team' as your measurable ROI. In this sort of situation, it might be difficult to persuade a third party to lend you money because the resultant growth might be too slow for them; they are more likely to want to see a quicker increase in profits. Choosing to self-finance an investment plan is easier and cheaper than trying to persuade a third party to lend and, although your growth might be slow, it might be worth it to you over a longer term (see also 'Lender', in Chapter 3, page 44). However, if a bank declines the opportunity to lend your business money, it would be wise to reflect on the reasons why – is your proposition really viable?

Business plan

Having a vision and a mission statement will help you in preparing a business plan, but they don't write the plan for you. There are many guides on how to write a business plan and what one should include, but even these won't necessarily make it any easier for you to actually start writing yours. Executive coaching can help you to develop a plan, using, say, the Business Model Canvas template (see 'Selection' in Chapter 2, page 25) or another prompt method.

Perhaps the hardest part of writing a business plan is to know who it is aimed at. It is commonly suggested the intended audience will be a bank or a funder – someone you would like to persuade to invest in your business. An alternative to help you get started would be to imagine you are writing it for a client or for a competition; you may be more familiar with this type of approach. In competition bids you might have to set out why you are the right choice for a particular type of work, describing how you have set up the business to be better than your competitors. When approaching clients, they may want to know what you are working towards, so they can see if it aligns with their future direction – for instance, this could be staff development. Another kickstarter could be to imagine you are addressing a potential collaborator – suggesting you would like to work with them jointly on new projects.

When making long-term business plans, you should use your creativity in the same way you would when converting a client's brief into a new building. Preparing your business plan is like preparing a feasibility study – use it to allow you to experiment and test ideas across shorter time scales. Not everything will work, but expect change and remain open to possibilities.

Ultimately, you simply need to state:

- what you want to do
- why you want to do it, and
- how you are going to be successful at it.

You can think of setting business goals almost like setting a budget (see 'Direction' above). With a budget, you set out how much you will spend on a range of things throughout the year and then periodically check to see how close you are to your intentions. This allows you to adjust your spending as necessary if you see any deviation from the budgeted amounts. Critically, it exposes where you are meeting your targets and where you are not, giving you a chance to take corrective action through some type of planned intervention.

In a small practice, it can be difficult to disassociate yourself from the company. This places additional burdens on you as the leader. A business has a separate legal identity, so it can be useful to think of it as a separate entity, which will have targets that need to be met to satisfy others. This can help across a whole range of activities, from asking clients for money to asking staff members to do their job in a particular way. If the company exists as a set of values and principles, set up in such a way as to deliver a projected outcome, it becomes a thing in itself, in which people can place their trust and belief – staff and clients alike, even you.

This provides the opportunity to focus the direction of the practice and give all staff the chance to get on board. To meet your firm's potential, you need all arrows pointing in the same direction. Do your staff share your goals? Do they even know what your targets are? More importantly, do you?

It can be incredibly rewarding to have these kinds of conversations with the people you work with, but it can be difficult, especially if those people work for you. Asking simple questions, such as 'What do you want?' and 'Where do you want to get to?' may prove challenging for both sides and will only be successful where an atmosphere of trust and understanding has been established. If you want people to be honest, they need to feel safe. The purpose of having the conversation at all needs to be understood, and the scope of what will and can be included also needs to be laid out and made clear at the outset; for every practice, this will be different. Whatever stage your business is at – whether newly opened, with a long history or already with a business plan – the benefit of establishing clarity of direction means you will know when you have achieved what you set out to do.

If it is the first time you have written one, or even if you have written several, your business plan will not be perfect, because it will have to adapt to the fact that everything changes. However, it will enable your practice to stay on track towards achieving what you set out to achieve.

Profile

Part of the Vision Orbit exercise (see the 'Strategy' box on page 6) is to ask yourself what is your favourite type of project. If you ask any architect this question, you can usually expect their response to include something about what a building looks like or how it was conceived, and words like 'simplicity', 'delight' and 'design', or 'contemporary', 'connection' and 'quality'. What you don't often hear is 'profitable'. This highlights a persistent problem among architects – practices are often *not* set up to be businesses that make money. If you asked another business the same question, you might expect them to say something different – perhaps the sort of work they want is work which allows them to sell more units at a better price. Architecture is not manufacturing or retailing, of course, but it is dependent on a client purchasing the architect's skill and time. The better you are at producing what the client wants, the simpler the task, and that normally means there is lower risk and less time spent, without any loss of quality. When added together, this equals more profit and longer-term resilience to disruption.

If part of a practice's ambition is to target a particular type of project over others, you need to have better expertise in the chosen field. A long-term strategy to obtain this expertise might be formed around a training programme (with a budget) to raise the level of skills available among existing staff. A shorter-term solution may be to prepare a recruitment campaign to search for someone who already has these skills – effectively buying in the skills required to meet the business target. The time required to meet this ambition should be drafted into a marketing plan that includes the following information:

- How the practice intends to win the preferred work in the first place; for example, through targeted advertising or promotional activity.
- The resulting benefits; such as increased exposure in a particular area, leading to a higher likelihood of winning exactly the sort of work you want to focus on in the future.
- A target for the increased profits the practice is expected to recover over the time period allowed for the whole initiative. If this is written into a business plan, the practice might seek to borrow the amount of money required to invest in the plan, with the return period being laid out in a funding programme.

Any marketing plan will adopt a range of methods for reaching new audiences. Social media marketing has the advantage of allowing catchment parameters to be quite accurate, allowing you to deliver your campaign message to particular audiences within tightly controlled boundaries.

PRACTICE INSIGHTS

Social media advertising

By Jason Clark, Director, DCA Public Relations Ltd, Plymouth

There are many social advertising platforms available, with Facebook, Twitter, LinkedIn and Instagram among the most common. Some are designed for specific audiences, e.g. LinkedIn is a professional network and good for business-to-business promotion and recruitment. Instagram is more visual, while Facebook is more community-focused. Advertising campaigns have a myriad of targeting options and can be structured by geography, demographics, interests, income, purchase behaviours – it's a long list, but you can hone your audience. Be clear what you want your campaign to achieve. Are you brand building, encouraging more visits to your website, driving video views, generating new leads? Think about how social advertising can support your clients. For example, a pre-application consultation can be virtual and hyper-targeted at people in the neighbourhood and you are likely to reach many more than through a traditional drop-in event.

There may be readers convulsing right now at the prospect of marketing their business, but is it so different from the sort of exercise any private developer may undertake before embarking on a construction project? The sort of development project that architects will undoubtedly be employed to help deliver – being the 'bought in skills and expertise', as it were.

Why is it often anathema to architects to view the prospect of planning their own business development along these lines? Perhaps it is something to do with our learning and understanding of professionalism. Architects no doubt have wide-ranging knowledge and skills geared towards solving complex problems, but these are rarely aimed towards business development, expansion or capital growth. Having these at the forefront of your mind will help you strengthen and advance your practice as a resilient business that can adapt to unforeseen stresses.

Among architects, there still seems to be a pervading sense of anxiety about advertising. Our profession is perhaps still confused by its relationship with clients, although this may be more applicable to smaller practices than larger ones. In any event, the society in which we trade no longer operates on the principles and mores of the 1920s, and to pretend it does or to hang on to the possibility of their revival is unrealistic. This is not to say that professional relationships are no longer based on trust and understanding, mutual respect and tolerance, because they are – we are still just people after all. But holding on to vestiges of an anachronistic version of professionalism which precludes direct advertising of your product will not help the advancement of your business, and it may not help the advancement of architecture in the long run either. We trade in a market dominated by service industries, and the provision of our expertise is how we hope to make a living. We cannot pay the rent with etiquette.

Fee earners

Within practices, staff are commonly differentiated as either fee earners or non-fee earners, but why? Everyone in the office has a role to play and everyone there is working to help the practice earn fees. Regarding staff in this way can lead to problems – it can be divisive and, by not accounting for work performed by everyone in the practice, it can mean you earn less than is possible. Throughout this guide, I use the terms 'fee earners' and 'non-fee earners' for simplicity, but where you see the phrase 'fee earners' be sure to keep in mind the following interpretation.

If you cut a cross-section through the staff in an architect's practice it will reveal a stratification of architectural qualifications (usually), from qualified architects down to Part 2 and Part 1 students. Non-architectural staff may also be qualified, perhaps to a high level. Such a cross-section might differentiate individuals by their experience, such as director, associate, project architect, job runner etc. It may also illustrate the mix of disciplines in the practice – such as architect, technologist and, maybe, planner or engineer in a bigger practice.

It is likely the majority of staff are architectural and make up the so-called fee earners, and non-architectural staff, who may provide a vitally important function in the office, make up only a small proportion of the workforce. When you examine the figures you find that the proportion of non-architectural staff is generally low. I think this limits opportunities for growth in architects' practices, for the reasons set out below.

For a practice of between five and 19 staff, the average ratio of fee earners to non-fee earners is eight to one (eight fee earners to every one non-fee earner).[3] When you look at small practices, those employing anywhere between one and nine people, the average ratio is even more weighted, at eleven to one.[4] If this is you, ask yourself if you are making the best use of everyone's time. Maybe you refer to your staff as being either part of the drawing office or admin, or even simply architects and support staff – whatever the terms used, looking at the people you employ and assessing the ratio of fee earners to non-fee earners might tell you how many people are directly earning fees through chargeable time, but it is not the best way to consider the value of work available from your staff.

This current ratio may be due, in part, to the email revolution. Consider back when letters needed to be typed and the post needed to be dealt with; it would have been inconceivable not to have a non-architectural member of staff to perform those tasks – a secretary, junior or whatever name they would go by, someone to carry out administrative duties. Contrast that with the ease with which communications have become accessible to everyone now and this could seem to consign the administration role to the past. If answering the phone, replying to emails or accessing files can all be done electronically by anyone (without them moving), or even be partly automated, why would you employ admin staff to do it? Try this reason: because they save you money and improve your productivity and, with the right investment, bring added value too.

It is possible to assess someone's efficiency, or their utilisation percentage, using time-recording software (see the 'Resource allocation' box in Chapter 2, page 34, for more on this) – all fee-earning staff will be keeping some form of time sheet (if not, you should skip to 'Time recording' in Chapter 2, page 26). What this figure won't necessarily tell you though is whether it represents value for money. However, this is relatively simple to assess. First, break down the different tasks that a fee earner has undertaken during their project work. Then, look at those activities and ask whether all of them needed to have been done by an architectural staff member? Include the 'in-between' tasks too, such as answering the phone, filing emails (both sent and received), selecting attachments to submit with a planning application or filing attachments from emails received from consultants. You will find there are a lot of actions that do not require a trained architect to perform them.

Architects are expensive. Architectural students are more economical, but even they are costly enough to mean they should be kept focused on fee-earning activities. And in any case, students are likely to be with you for only a short time, depending on their grade (Part 1 for one year, Part 2 hopefully for three to four years), which means they may not have time to learn the complexities of some of these in-between tasks along with everything else they have to learn during their training years.

These in-between tasks are no less important as supporting activities, so you should consider the benefits to be gained from allocating them to non-architectural staff. The first is that the cost to the business could be less. Here there is a double benefit, because if you have a member of your non-architectural staff trained to carry out in-between tasks, your architectural staff can work on other architect-specific activities. The second is that these tasks occur repeatedly, if not always consecutively. One of the hardest things to make efficient is the carrying out of different tasks that all take a short amount of time. When you have to bill an architect's time against this type of work, it doesn't always prove to be cost-effective.

If a non-architectural member of staff has the flexibility to perform these tasks in between their general day-to-day duties, and is trained and encouraged to do so, the efficiency of the architectural staff can be improved, or at least maintained. However, because non-architectural staff time is not normally recorded or billed, this improvement in the fee earners' efficiency is not normally charged to specific projects; instead, it sinks into the practice's overheads. (Support staff, administrators or non-fee earners are normally allocated as an overhead to the business, which is paid for by fees earned.) These activities do frequently offer value to a project, however, and should be charged accordingly. If they are recognised as a task being undertaken by a member of your staff who is trained to do so – one who is offering specific value to the project – the work can and should be costed, e.g. as a lump sum, and charged to the client, a bit like an expense.

The third benefit is that the member of staff selected to carry out these tasks will develop new skills – not only is their development being invested in, which means their confidence and capacity grow, but you will also create a specialist in a particular role. Many of the tasks, such as uploading applications to the Planning Portal, can grow in complexity over time, perhaps as planning authorities make changes to their criteria, or a specific software company introduces updates, with online training seminars to assist users. As the tasks grow, so the time needed to invest in them also grows – meaning even more time would be taken from architectural staff. As your non-architectural staff member's skill increases in these areas, so their expertise also develops. With the right encouragement, they can become the expert in the room, able to advise on what is or isn't needed – in a planning application, say, or how and when to request information at the start of a new project.

Many of these so-called in-between tasks are repetitive – the same requirement might occur on a number of jobs, with little to distinguish them from each other. Most of them do not require specific design skills, but they do require a different set of skills – not always possessed by architects and architectural students. The 'soft skills' required to chase up a consultant for a report, for instance, or answering the phone to a client, or even liaising with a local authority for an extension to a deadline, are not always abundant in architects and architectural staff (some may disagree) (see 'Reporting' in Chapter 5, page 81). Where there are repeating processes, such as for obtaining competitive quotations from suppliers, they can be simplified and improved if done in a systematic way. Establishing methods or checklists for such tasks can be easily taught to non-architectural staff.

People tend to have a natural proclivity towards certain methods of working – selecting the right person for the right task need not mean they do this to the exclusion of all else, just that the work of the practice is spread out between all staff. This is not a new idea, of course. Adam Smith wrote about the division of labour in the late 18th century, when he said cooperation between workers in a specific industry would result in increased production.[5] If architects working in practice are employed to answer the phone, prepare all their own emails, file everything to do with their own projects, is this is the best use of the practice's resources? Using more expensive staff to carry out work that could be done by others can also put unnecessary pressure on staff time – if they have architectural work to complete, this can be taxing enough, but couple that with a responsibility to undertake all the administrative duties as well, and that may put undue pressure on their uncontracted hours or result in simple mistakes being made.

Once you understand the mechanics of your business in this way, you can utilise more accurately the resources you have available, which means you are more likely to be profitable. You will also be better able to respond quickly to emerging trends or react rapidly to situations that might affect you – this is what will make your business more resilient to threats. Embedding this knowledge into a resource plan means you can take advantage of the so-called unproductive time. You can use it to contribute to the wider growth of the business over the longer term.

Technology

Analysing the time records for individual projects, especially those within similar sectors or of comparable scale, reveals the actual amount of time taken to reach each invoice stage. Using this data to calculate the true cost of a project for your practice gives you the information needed to decide what your fee bid should be for similar work in the future.

Over the past decade, many offices have shifted away from using analogue time-recording methods and are instead embracing digital management systems that can combine time recording with invoicing. When information is held on a spreadsheet, it usually needs to be manually copied over to a separate spreadsheet ledger to allow management accounts to be prepared. Web-based systems automatically connect pieces of information, to allow much quicker reporting and analysis. However, it can take a full year or more to make a switch like this, where invoicing and accounts are involved, due to the need to keep a consistent record for filing accounts at the end of the financial year. The transition process may take up to 18 months in smaller practices.

Identifying and trialling new software, whether a replacement accounting package or new CAD system, can be implemented from the top or led by staff input. Conducting reviews with staff and providing a platform for discussion on how regular tasks are performed can help you identify where there are opportunities for improvement. Staff who follow advances in new technology may bring new software to everyone else's attention, offering a way to change the way you do things.

It is always worth looking into new ways of doing things, but you must consider seriously the risk that you may, in the future, lose the ability to access some of the data being entered into a new platform. Information recorded about a project needs to be available for a long time after the project has been finished,[6] but it is not guaranteed the new platform or app you are considering will be available for ever. Don't use this as a reason to avoid change, however, as most new programmes include an export function for data.

The critical question when considering investing in any new technology is not always 'What will we get out of it?' but 'What do we have to put into it?' If you are going to get out less than you put in, it clearly isn't going to be worth it. It is not always going to be possible to know this, but it is worth scenario planning a few instances to test and, if they pass, running a few trials.

Technology has become such an integral part of our lives that it is impossible to imagine a working day without interacting with it. We are all so familiar with the automation of repetitive tasks when using our everyday software. However, it can be easy to overlook the fact that these programmes can usually do more than we ask them to. If you were to check how different staff members prepare simple documents in, say, Microsoft Word, you would probably find each person would do it differently, e.g. using bullets, tables or tabs. This is not going to make much difference generally, until somebody else has to edit a document or add something to it. That person then has to spend time adjusting the document to make it work for them. If this happens regularly, over days, weeks or months, it can add up to a surprising amount of wasted time. Do not fall into the trap of thinking this only applies to members of staff who are not 'young' – there is still an expectation (among older people) that young people know how to use all software simply because they are young; this is simply not the case.

The task of considering what new software to purchase can be daunting, given the amount that is available. First, though, you have to decide whether or not it is even going to be worth your while investing resources in it. The best and only way to manage this process is by booking in time to discuss the issues with other staff members. Everyone will interact with existing and new software at some point, so gathering as much input as possible at the early stages is going to highlight, at the very least, when and where attention needs to be focused. It does not make sense to replace everything at the same time, if only because of the disruption it would cause. However, from time to time it can be useful to have a root and branch review of all software used, and to draft a phased plan about how and when (or if) it needs to be changed. This can become part of the Vision Orbit exercise, or simply be added straight into the business plan.

CYBERSECURITY

Following the outbreak of the coronavirus pandemic in 2020, the use of technology accelerated again, catalysed by the move to working from home, in line with the government guidance issued at the time. The rush to hastily establish remotely accessed networks and mobile equipment will have left many firms vulnerable to cyber attacks. Almost overnight, firewalls and network passwords, and all the previously accepted protocols for keeping information safely on computers hardwired into an office server, became relaxed out of necessity.

Most malicious activity usually results from simple breaches in security. Therefore, any disruption to an established office-based set-up that results in the use of private links, different versions of operating system software and out-of-date passwords will place the business at risk. There are strict codes detailing the timetable for reporting any data breaches that have occurred. These are controlled through the Information Commissioner's Office,[7] to which all businesses are legally required to pay an annual fee. That is not to say there is widespread protection for businesses who have been targeted. Instead, it is not uncommon to hear of victims who have been forced to pay some kind of ransom, often in a cryptocurrency, to recover access to their own data. Cybersecurity threats are now beginning to be excluded from professional indemnity insurance policies, as a new specialist market to provide cover for this kind of risk is emerging (see 'Insurance broker' in Chapter 3, page 52).

Simple technology audits and frequent password updates across all staff computers represent basic, common-sense measures for providing low-level security. These measures would be in addition to the business's obligation under the General Data Protection Regulation (GDPR) to implement protection of data. Online file storage is often regarded as being more secure than office-based, hard disc storage devices, due to the encryption of data when accessing the subscribed-to facilities and the fact that they are not vulnerable to petty theft, fire or water damage from leaks.

To ensure you have at least the minimum level of protection for any files and client data contained within project databases, you should undertake a wholesale review of access to this information, followed by regular assessments.

It is also important to give consideration to a disaster recovery plan, so there is a procedure in place to be adopted if the worst were to happen. If an incident does occur, and immediate action is required, the ability to think clearly and with a cool logic is severely tested, so having a plan in place will be invaluable. Such a plan can cover other catastrophic situations, such as flood, fire or burglary. It can be sobering to reflect on these possibilities, but if the solutions have already been laid out, it can be surprisingly quick to re-establish a trading position.

Endnotes

1 Gerhard, F., Laurent, M.-P., Spyrounakos, K. and Windhagen, E. 'Next-generation nowcasting to improve decision making in a crisis' (McKinsey & Company, 2021). Available at: https://www.mckinsey.com/business-functions/risk-and-resilience/our-insights/next-generation-nowcasting-to-improve-decision-making-in-a-crisis [accessed 16 December 2021].

2 Pinder-Ayres, B. *Financial Management* (London: RIBA Publishing, 2016).

3 Figures extrapolated by Adrian Malleson from the RIBA Business Benchmarking 2021 survey data, representing 42,308 practice staff.

4 Calculated from an assessment of 2,887 practices.

5 Munger, M. 'Division of Labor, Part 1', Adam Smith Works, 7 August 2019. Available at: https://www.adamsmithworks.org/documents/division-of-labor-part-1 [accessed 10 August 2021].

6 Limitation periods under UK law are set out in the Limitation Act 1980. The time limit within which a claim can be made under a simple contract signed under hand is six years; for a contract that is signed under seal or deed, the time limit is 12 years. Where a mistake has been made, the time period will not start until the claimant has discovered the mistake. For time periods relating to latent injury through negligence (e.g. where knowledge of the right to claim is discovered after the cause of action occurred), the time limit can be three years or six years, depending on the circumstances, but in either case the action must be brought within 15 years from when the negligent act occurred. For all such matters, legal advice should be obtained.

7 Information Commissioner's Office. *Responding to a cybersecurity incident: How and when to report a cybersecurity incident to the ICO* (Wilmslow: ICO, 2021). Available at: https://ico.org.uk/media/for-organisations/documents/2614816/responding-to-a-cybersecurity-incident.pdf [accessed 16 December 2021].

2

Projects

There is not just one way to run a successful business – nobody will tell you it is better to choose one model over another or to choose only commercial clients over domestic. When you run a business, however, you should make a decision about what you are doing it for and where you are taking it. Unless you are clear about these things you run the risk of drifting. To be resilient you need to have a clear sense of purpose and direction. This is not at odds with being open and willing to consider changing direction or taking on alternative clients and projects; all opportunities can be considered. Within a structure of sound decision-making, backed up by evidence, your business has more chance of remaining stable. From this position you can respond to unexpected changes in direction or consider what direction you want to travel in next. Only you will know if you enjoy your work more when you make more money or when you complete a project in the way you want to, or whether working with one type of client over another is more rewarding.

Having a clearly defined business plan and a strategy for delivering a shared vision communicates to your staff where you want to go and what you are doing to get there. This message can be understood by those outside the practice as well, and contributes to building a business identity. These things matter when it comes to promoting your services. They define your marketing strategy, and help you carve a new route towards something you choose to explore next. Armed with your direction, purpose and growth proposition, you can plan to work on the projects you want while continuing to run a resilient organisation.

Sectors

Look for profitability in every aspect of your business. Find ways to squeeze as much out of the basics as possible. For instance, if you see a trend developing in a certain type of project work – either a drop in efficiency or an increase in the number of projects – explore what it might signify? From a vision-planning exercise, you may have identified a sector in which to expand, which could be valuable to your practice.

At different points throughout the year, you will be required to assemble a list of projects you have worked on and to categorise them into different sectors. It is a useful exercise, but it can also be quite daunting if you stop to consider the many conflicting lists of sectors available. Consider the following examples, which you are likely to come into contact with in any given year.

- If you are a RIBA Chartered Practice, you will be obliged to complete the annual RIBA Business Benchmarking survey. Since this was introduced, there have been several changes to the order and nature of the survey questions, as different organisations have been awarded the role of collecting the survey data. This has meant the list of sector headings has also changed over the time the survey has been in operation.
- If you advertise your practice through 'Find an Architect' on the RIBA website, you will be asked to select all the different sectors you have experience of working in.
- It is normal for the annual renewal form for your professional indemnity insurance to request an assessment of the sectors you have worked in (by percentage of jobs worked on) over the past year. Many insurance brokers still use quite old-fashioned forms (Figure 2.1 gives an example of a professional indemnity insurance renewal form from 2013, in which a question on grades of staff shows the dated nature of the language used by some insurers – see: '(e) Typists/Office Boys'). Consequently, the lists of sectors might not quite match up with any list you may write for yourself. However, persuading insurance companies and brokers to adjust their procedures to suit yours seems like a battle not worth fighting.

	Please state number of:					
21	(a)	Partners/Directors/Principals	1	(d)	Trainee Staff	
	(b)	Qualified Staff	2	(e)	Typists/Office Boys	
	(c)	Draughtsmen	1	(f)	All other Staff	2 ADMIN – P/T 1 CLEANER – P/T

Figure 2.1: Extract from a professional indemnity insurance renewal form from 2013, showing the dated nature of the language used

In addition to these published lists, you either will already have or will create your own lists from the records of projects undertaken by your practice.
You will also use sectors when preparing marketing plans, especially when highlighting those which you are aiming to break into. Looking at all these sector names in the round, with the various available options, provides an opportunity for you to agree a straightforward way of labelling the project sectors relevant to your practice.

When preparing your own list of sectors, keep it simple and appropriate to the work you do and seek to do – for example, 'residential' can be broken down to a granular level, but how many different types of residential projects do you actually work on? How different from one another are they? How different do they need to be for you to be able to make use of the data? Once you have your own list, you can establish a simple table that cross-references your descriptions against those on the published lists and in forms that you will need to return annually. This will not only speed up the process of filling in the forms, but will also help in other ways.

Each time you take a new enquiry, assess what sector the project is likely to fall into and attach your practice's agreed sector name to the details. If this information is taken through to the actual job folder (assuming you convert the prospect into a new project), this will provide you with a growing register of searchable sectors, allowing you to access any other information you collect within job folders, such as fee quotes, time spent and invoices issued. It doesn't take long to have enough information on different sectors to allow more detailed and useful analysis of the data.

Simple procedural protocols introduced into your day-to-day administration activities should be designed to provide you with the data-mining capability to allow you to establish hard facts about projects. For instance, you might prefer to work on certain types of project only to find they are not as profitable as other types. This doesn't mean you should stop doing them, it just means you become aware of the cost to the practice and make decisions knowing the consequences.

Sector information may also come from your social media activities. You can count the 'likes' on your Facebook page for projects grouped within a sector you have chosen to promote, or you can keep a record of the increase in engagements or impressions on your social media generally whenever those projects are posted.

This is your business's unique information, and the more accessible to searches you can make it, the more valuable it becomes in helping you make decisions. Monitor regularly to see if it changes and, when it does, be flexible enough to adapt your business plan to accommodate it.

Scale

Being able to balance the projects you agree to take on with your capacity to complete them in a timely fashion is an important consideration. Architects are bound by the Architects Code[1] (regulated by the Architects Registration Board) to ensure you can adequately resource the work you agree to undertake. Standard 4 of the code states:

> 4.2 You should ensure that you are able to provide adequate professional, financial and technical resources when entering into a contract and throughout its duration.

What matters most about projects when they are in the office is the time they take to complete, and large projects don't always equal long projects. Large projects tend to keep you busy, and while they require more drawings, more staff and more resources, they don't tend to waste as much time proportionally as small projects. When a project takes a long time to complete it can put severe downward pressure on profitability. It is difficult not to waste time on small projects, and even harder to get paid for all the time taken. This is because small projects have the same points to consider along the way, such as client approvals, local authority permissions and costings, resulting in disproportionately long periods of time waiting for other parties between short periods of time spent working on the project.

To assess the contribution that small projects can make to the practice, you should assess their value from different perspectives. You can then choose how many you want in your forward order book and define what part they have to play in your business plan.

For example, micro projects might not increase your fee income substantially, but they have a role to play in the education of students. Trainee staff will learn a lot from doing them, although you may have to allocate a lot of their time to a 'house account' in their time sheet for their training. If you have already set a budget for this as part of your business plan, the value becomes worth it, but if not, it could become a drain. The value gained from nurturing skills and confidence in a student architect on a small commission actually has little to do with profit, but can instead bring almost tangible joy. Their journey through a project stage and their satisfaction when they have completed it successfully makes the 'cost' worth it. Growing the capacity of a member of staff is infectious and raises the spirits of a team like nothing else – that's priceless, isn't it?

This is not dissimilar from the satisfaction gained from providing a client or prospective client with sound advice, taken directly from your expertise, even if it does not actually result in work coming into the office. Here, the value can be cashed in as reputation. Providing solid advice to those local to your practice premises will promote the kind of conversations you want members of the public to be having about your business, ones where words like integrity, honesty and professionalism are used. If you compare the cost of one or two hours of your time spent helping someone benefit from your experience against the cost of an advert in the local paper, the value is clearly within budget.

Notwithstanding, it is possible to extract profit from small-scale projects. There is a special kind of discipline required to chop and change between lots of small jobs though, and keeping them all moving forward, without stalling – especially when each stage of the work only takes a few days, or even a few hours – requires no small level of skill. When the cost of each hiatus is equivalent to, or more than, the cost of the stage task itself, the time it takes to manage the project along its journey can be disproportionate to the value of the whole commission. It is perhaps ironic that, to be profitable, the smallest projects usually require those with the most expertise and experience to complete them quickly, in one sitting. They can sometimes be fun too!

Selection

Mapping your practice's past projects over time is a simple way to identify what types of project make you the most money – remember, you are in business to make money. Taking time to choose the types of projects to take on might make you more money. The key word here is 'choose': you should choose where you want to focus your efforts to seek new work, whether on the basis of sector or scale, or perhaps some other factor, such as location (as some places are more affluent than others, so offer more opportunities for making a profit). Once you make a decision to target a particular type of work, your resources should be focused on making it happen.

Choosing what work you want your practice to do, or what work you don't want to do, could be seen as a luxury – and when work is scarce, it might really feel like it. If, however, you have a strategic aim to work on projects of a certain size, within a specific sector or in a chosen location, being choosy can be the right approach, even when work is thin on the ground. From your analysis of the sectors in which you work (see 'Sectors', above), you will know the type and range of different projects you work on, and you may even have an idea how profitable each one is in comparison to the others.

The Business Model Canvas management tool (a method first proposed by Alexander Osterwalder of Strategyzer) asks you to consider your revenue streams – or, put simply, where does your money come from and in what proportions? When this information is attributed to the projects you work on in different sectors, you begin to build a very simple but powerful dataset on the potential growth of your business. This means you can make an informed decision on where you want your practice to go. Do you know, for instance, whether you make more money from an extension, a new build or a conversion? Comparing the profits from the different project groups (as a percentage of the total cost invested in each one) will soon tell you – and is a relatively straightforward calculation. Targeting projects that suit your practice's specific skill sets, which have been borne out by the numbers, will drive up fee income and improve profitability.

Setting out your strategic aims should take these matters into consideration. Are you really choosing work that suits your aims and objectives for your practice? Or are you taking on whatever work comes your way? When you think about what work you want to encourage into your practice, you need to be asking yourself: what do you want to be known for and what are you good at? What skills do you have available already within your staff and what can you obtain? If you haven't already audited your staff to assess their latent, and possibly underused, skill sets, this might be the time to do so (see more on staff in Chapter 4).

Being able to choose when to take on one job over another requires information, conviction and ambition – plus a certain amount of courage. This is helped by having a strategic plan, which is best prepared with the rest of your staff – if they are on board with you, everyone's job becomes easier. If everyone agrees the intention for the business, they are more likely to want to be part of it. For them to know this, though, requires the plan to be available to them and for it to be understood. But be aware, undertaking these business planning exercises can result in some members of your staff deciding they don't agree, at which point they will have to make a decision whether to stay or go. This will be a test of the strength of your belief in the vision and the mission for the practice, and a test of your strength as a leader too.

Ultimately, decisions about direction rest with the leader of the organisation. Just like planning a new development, you can assemble a file brimful with context analysis to inform you of the opportunities and constraints inherent within the site, but at some point you have to choose where to put the building on the ground. This is your judgement call, made using experience and skill. Making a decision in business is the same – gather the information and call it. If you have good information, which is reliable, current and relevant, you will survive.

Time recording

There's no escaping it – time sheets are the be all and end all of practice, yet even though they are the easiest things in the world to prepare, they are hands down the easiest things to put off. As Brian Pinder-Ayres puts it:

> The detailed recording of time is one of those administrative activities that does not come easily to many architects.[2]

The digital time-recording software packages that are now available (see the 'Case studies' box on page 37 for some examples) enable more detailed analysis of times recorded than is possible using analogue systems, which may themselves often just be adaptations of manual time sheets loaded onto spreadsheets – analogous to the way CAD drawings might be seen as lines drawn using a computer rather than a pen, and Building Information Modelling (BIM) drawings as intelligent, digital models. However, with the additional interpretation ability usually comes a corresponding requirement to prepare time records more frequently, to make best use of the data and the facility to analyse it. With analogue systems, time sheets may only needed to be handed in weekly, while it is not uncommon for digital recording to be completed daily, so that records can constantly be kept up to date and the status of any and all projects shown as quickly as possible. Therefore, whatever can be done to make the actual task of recording time simpler should be seized upon (remember, this may include non-architectural staff too, as noted under 'Fee earners' in Chapter 1, page 14). Helping staff to get their time sheets done will help everyone else too, especially those involved with invoicing.

Most digital systems will allow their settings to be customised, meaning you can set them up in the manner most suited to your office systems (or to new systems you wish to introduce). It is common among practices to record time against the RIBA Plan of Work stages, so if stages can be preset for each project, not only will it make it easier for users to enter their times, but it will also reduce the possibility of time being recorded against the wrong stage. This is important whether the billing is on a time-spent basis, a lump-sum amount by percentage of work complete or any other method, because to be of maximum value the time record needs to be available for review in the future. It becomes the best method you have to determine how long a piece of work actually took. If the work element recorded is broken down into RIBA Plan of Work stages, it is significantly more useful to you when reviewing the project or when pricing another similar job.

Depending on the system, it may be possible to set up other preset options. If so, a list of the activities most likely to be carried out by the person recording their time can be created for them to select from. This will result in the recorder having fewer choices to make, and only one piece of variable data to add – their actual time spent. More importantly, it makes it possible to compare the work that is actually being done against what was supposed to be done, giving an early warning to the 'fee-killer' that is scope creep (explored further later in this chapter).

When setting up a preset dropdown list of activities for time sheets, as well as listing the activities you have been commissioned to deliver you should also include an option for additional work. This makes it possible to undertake time analysis of the project to show if there is any overspend relative to project budgets, giving you the chance to steer a wayward project back on track.

If your principal use for time sheets is to enable invoicing, you should review your systems to ensure that everything helps the billing process to be carried out as quickly and easily as possible. The life cycle of a project is pretty much the same for every project, even though you may do different work for different projects. It goes like this:

Enquiry → Fee proposal → Agreement → Activity → Time record → Invoice

Provided the *activity* is done in accordance with the agreed *fee proposal*, the *invoice* will almost always be paid. Easy ... right? It should be, and if we were simply selling rivets, it might be. But when we are rendering services, there is seemingly always a need for more interpretation. (Incidentally, notice how the fee-earning work element – the *activity* – is only part of the project's life cycle.) Let's look more closely at the association between just these three parts of the project life cycle:

Fee proposal → Time record → Invoice

If you can use the same information in all three parts, you really will simplify the process. The more closely your time records match the fee proposal, the easier it will be for you to prepare the invoice.

Keeping accurate time records is one of the most important things you can do in your business. They will show you everything, from what you should charge on one project to how much to quote on another. They must be accurate, and the level of detail needs to be proportionate – they must also be useable and staff must be able to complete them efficiently.

If you set out your initial fee proposal in a manner that can be reproduced in the settings of your time-recording software or spreadsheet – as a list of services the practice will be commissioned to provide – this will simplify the time-recording process. It will both limit the information that will need to be entered and ensure that time is recorded for each service the client has commissioned. The time records can then be transposed directly onto the client's invoice, so they will see the cost for each service they agreed to pay for. This also makes it easier for time sheets to be completed quickly and invoices to be issued promptly, meaning there is more chance you will be paid on time – which will increase your assets, reduce your working capital (see Chapter 1) and make the business more profitable.

Time sheets also supply the information required for the preparation of a work in progress (WIP) calculation. This is critical in providing a picture of the practice's profitability at any point in time because it quantifies the fees due (current assets). In simple terms:

WIP = fees earned – fees invoiced

You will need to calculate WIP annually, for your end-of-year accounts. However, calculating it on a more regular basis can provide helpful snapshots of where the practice's efforts are being spent. The warning here is that, although it is the practice's aggregate record of fees 'earned', WIP does not always equal the fees due. Unless you track and respond to the overspend on time recorded against a project minute by minute, the WIP figure will include this overspend. Tracking so closely is unrealistic, but monitoring the overspend through better use of time sheets can produce project analytics relatively quickly and easily.

Critically, remember that you will always carry a certain amount of WIP – if the value of your WIP is zero, you're either insolvent or on the verge of it! WIP is effectively a running total of the value of work waiting to be invoiced. The amount of WIP reflects the number of people you have working and how efficient they are – the appropriate amount to carry is a function of the frequency at which you invoice and the terms you offer your debtors.

PRACTICE INSIGHTS

Forward planning

By Paula Willmore, Founder Director, Willmore Iles Architects Ltd, Bristol

We are now in the process of looking at WIP for all projects. This will allow us to look at monthly activity against fees invoiced. We have also taken on a financial consultant, David Norgrove, initially to work for us three days a week for six to eight months to sharpen up our financial data. We recognised that as a company of 27 people and turnover of approximately £2 million, we needed to take our financial reporting to the next level.

With the planned retirement of our practice manager, we have a new practice manager who is much more engaged with our time-recording software, Deltek. We are now using Deltek far more effectively than before. We are in the process of updating all the historical information. We have also now started a succession planning project called WIA 2.0 – Leadership Challenge, which involves training up the next generation Senior Leadership Team to take over at the point when the two founder directors leave in a few years' time.

Records

The keeping of accurate records is an important discipline for any business. For an architecture practice, records can be particularly important as there is always the possibility of being sued by a client for negligence. If this happens to your practice, you will find that any time taken up by record-keeping has been time well spent. Of course, having project records will not prevent you from being sued if an allegation against you is taken further, but they will certainly help you to defend yourself.

As well as keeping project records, it is also useful to make records of other activities undertaken in the office. For example, a phone log – where the time of all incoming calls is recorded alongside who they are from and who they are for – can prove invaluable in any project investigation you may be called on to make. Phone logs may be simple, but they are incredibly effective for assembling a timeline for events. Ideally, you will be able to generate a phone log automatically by using a digital system, but in our office we haven't been able to list out the information we need, so we still use a day diary. A 'post in/post out' book is now rarely used, mainly because so little actual post is sent these days, but it is useful to record dates and details of any post that is sent out.

Having records will also help you in your day-to-day work, not just when you are facing the threat of a claim. For example, keeping a daily note of the weather can provide a very quick way to assess a contractor's claim for an extension of time due to inclement weather – again, we simply note this in a day diary.

Being in the habit of noting down basic project information, such as people, firms, changes and events, makes it easier to review quickly what happened during a project's lifetime. It will also form part of your health and safety, Construction (Design and Management) (CDM) Regulations and quality control measures and help you to improve your services. It might also protect the firm from challenges by demonstrating the level of organisation, care and attention you pay to each project. Being able to produce detailed information on a project's history in a simple format is evidence of a professional approach, which reflects on the credibility and reliability of the practice.

As for the project records themselves, they must be sufficiently brief to prevent record-keeping becoming burdensome, and they must be meticulously filed to ensure you can find them. Ideally, they should be centrally located, so that any member of staff can always access them. The use of a construction collaboration system – such as Viewpoint, Procore or ProjectSight (available at the time of writing) – will enable you to assemble documents for multiple projects in specific locations, allowing easy access to files, reports or photographs and for project notes to be kept with each project. These systems tend to come into their own when projects are on site – if a project is small, or is unlikely to go beyond building regulations approval, or even planning, they may be a bit excessive. Some time-keeping software systems, such as Synergy, Deltek and CMap, provide a form of consolidated project note facility, where notes are filed specifically under the project they relate to, which may be sufficient for your practice's needs. Even creating a shared spreadsheet in Google Workspace or SharePoint will provide a centralised location for recording information on each project that can then be assessed by another team member.

Any notes added to the project records must include the author's name, the date and the specific project's unique reference. Important matters to record include:

- changes in scope
- client's instructions and questions
- builder's requests and comments
- other specific items of information, such as feedback from the planning or building regulation authorities.

SCOPE CREEP

Accurate and comprehensive project records will be hard to argue against should you find yourself facing the threat of 'scope creep'. Deemed the 'killer of profit', this phenomenon is lethal in the way it stealthily slides into your staff time sheets and then bursts out of the figures, revealing its inexorable demands on everyone's attention but refusing to be squeezed into those carefully programmed stage fee targets. The incremental nature of its domination is what makes it so difficult to bring under control and the only effective measure against it once it has appeared is to swoop down onto it and stifle its growth immediately. The best way to prevent it ever getting into the office, though, is to be merciless in the way you set out your fee bid. Make it abundantly clear to all clients at the outset that any work they request that is not covered in the fee bid – such as redesign work for issued drawings –will be charged as 'extra services'. The importance of this simply cannot be overstated.

Ask clients as many questions as you can at the briefing, however obvious they seem, and ask for copies of as much information as they hold, especially on domestic projects – and make a note of all the questions they were asked. Throughout the project it can also be useful to record those marginal comments that people sometimes make and which can illustrate the way they are thinking, possibly acting as early warning indicators. Notes such as these are especially useful if centrally filed. They can give other members of the team a heads-up on how different actors within the project are feeling – whether they are becoming frustrated, changing the scope, or have started to refer to some new information you did not previously know about, such as a pre-existing survey.

Remaining on the lookout for any signs that give away a person's state of mind can be crucial in heading off potential conflicts or disputes. When such signs appear, it is sensible to act on them straight away. This might involve simply making a call to that person to ask if everything is alright, arranging a project update meeting, or getting everyone around the table for a discussion on issues and problems that need resolving. Indeed, this is part of the role of the architect – the lead figure between the client and their project, liaising with all consultants, builders and authorities. Tackling issues as they come up isn't always easy, but it is always easier than unpicking a situation later, especially when you did previously have time for an intervention.

Clients are guaranteed to become frustrated if they have to ask you for something more than once or if they believe you have included something they specifically said they didn't want. They will not want to pay for the time you spend making corrections, and may demand a discount if you have to undo something they are convinced they had already made clear. It is therefore important that all discussions and communications with clients are properly recorded.

Keeping a note of every comment, request or instruction made is practically impossible and unrealistic, but using annotations on drawings alongside meeting notes can be effective and speedy. Making notes during meetings and summarising the actions agreed before the end of the meeting allows everyone to add anything they feel is important that has been missed off the list.

Taking particular care to note down the obvious can be helpful for the future. It is often the case, when looking back over historical meeting notes, that you can't find something you are convinced was said. It is easy not to write something down because it seemed so obvious at the time, but these are exactly the notes you need. To counter this, think about the information required to review a project, or to familiarise yourself with an ongoing one you are about to become involved in. Under these 'safe' conditions – i.e. when you are not perilously close to being sued – you can think clearly about the crucial information you need. This can then form part of a guide for note-taking during live projects.

Alternatively, think about writing notes for someone else to read later. Assume the person is not part of the project and so doesn't know the context and is not familiar with the details. This is the situation you will find yourself in when you are being asked to review a historical project if an allegation has been made against your practice. At that point, you may be investigating a project you didn't work on or which you worked on so long ago that you can't recall its details precisely. Even if you can remember the fundamental information, if there are no records then it may not prove to be as valuable to your defence as it could have been.

Although perhaps a little dramatic, try to imagine how you would answer the judge when they look down at you in the dock and ask you why you didn't act on the information. It will get you into the habit of noting down what you need to protect yourself.

Resourcing

Analysing time spent by different staff members shows you their true availability to work on projects. It reveals how much time they spend on project work and how much they are 'unproductive'; as you will see, their 'productive' time is not always as much as you think.

Choosing who will do what and when is a complex programming task. It is governed by a significant number of competing factors, most especially: what is the cost of choosing to do one thing before another? For instance, if work on site is delayed because you haven't supplied information in a timely manner, the cost can be significantly more than if you miss a deadline for the submission of an application to the local authority. Resource planning is essentially a never-ending risk assessment, in which you have to balance a series of competing demands on your time and the time your staff have available. You must also predict how much time each task or activity is likely to take, and then cross your fingers in hope that it ends up taking no more than the amount of time you have available, both in terms of physical hours on the clock and the remaining chargeable time left in the fee agreement. And then there are the live events which scupper all best-laid plans – it is commonly said a programme is out of date the moment it is issued.

Preparing an office programme that includes all this information can be a daunting undertaking, so it helps to establish as much as you can before you make a start on the substantive part of the work. Much of the information can be worked out beforehand, to reduce the variables when planning. The amount of information you expect to get out of the programme will determine how complex it needs to be. You might be satisfied with just the allocation of time for specific staff over a period of a week or month, or you might want to see the next invoicing date, RIBA Plan of Work stage or percentage of completion of a specific activity. Depending on the scope and scale of the project, the increments of time being planned out may vary from a few hours to days or, even, months.

In the section 'Scale' above, I referred to the amount of time it is possible to waste. This can be worked out to a degree for your office programme. In any given year, you or your employees will have time off for holidays, sickness and training, be involved in non-fee-earning work and also (yes, it is true) waste a certain amount of time. You could call this 'unrecoverable time', or anything else, but what you can't do is expect everyone to work 100% of the time every day – it's unrealistic and, even if they could, it would only be for a short time because it's unsustainable. Knowing what units of time you have available among your paid staff to distribute between your different projects is step one in resource programming.

RESOURCE ALLOCATION

One architect employee contracted to work 9 am to 5.30 pm, five days a week, is providing you with 1,950 hours a year. They are required to keep a time sheet, attend staff meetings and contribute to general office duties – such as making tea or coffee, answering the phone and filing emails (but also see 'Fee earners', in Chapter 1, page 14). Let's say that takes up around 4 to 5 hours a week, which means you can allocate them to provide around 6.5 hours a day of productive work. Yes, but not for the whole year. Each year they are entitled to a minimum of 5.6 weeks of holiday (including bank holidays), which is 210 hours. They are required to undertake 35 hours of continuing professional development (CPD), plus 2.5 hours of health and safety training. They might be sick for a week, so that's another 37.5 hours gone, and if you deduct their 4 to 5 hours of unrecoverable time for the period when they are working, i.e. not when they are on holiday or sick, their 1,950 hours have now reduced down to around 1,445 to 1,490 hours, or about 75% of the time for which you pay them to work for you. If they have other duties, such as management, their percentage goes down even more.

In your resourcing allocation, you now know you have this architect for around 6.5 hours a day, but not always for the full week, depending on their other entitlements. In terms of the overall picture, if you make similar calculations for all of your staff, including yourself, the amount of productive time can be accurately plotted (to a degree – you obviously won't be able to programme when someone will be ill). If you, as the manager, expect to provide 6.5 hours of productive time each day regularly, you are either bionic or ignoring other things, such as general practice matters, business duties or your own health and wellbeing. Figure 2.2 shows an example of a practice director's 'utilisation' over a period of 11 months, taken from a time-recording software system called Synergy.

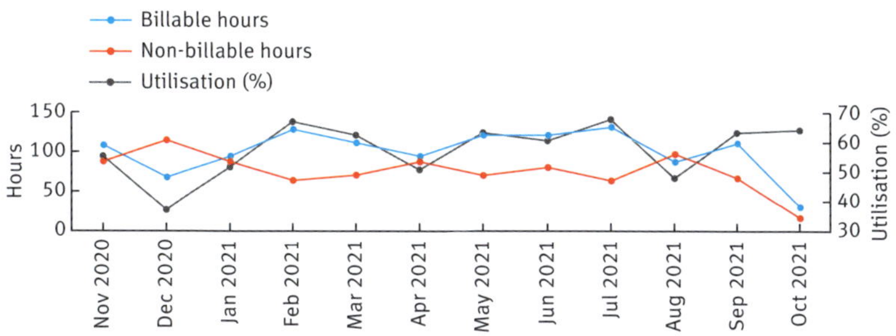

Figure 2.2: Practice director's work utilisation graph between November 2020 and October 2021, taken from Synergy time-recording software

You can see in Figure 2.2 how the amount of fee-earning time available for a director of practice over a long period can vary between about 35% and 65%. Gathering information like this provides valuable data for budgeting your resources over the year. It also highlights how much project work you need if you are to keep all the resources you have available occupied, or how much you are short by. This straightforward prediction process can provide your business with an early warning system, to alert you to either a shortage of work or a shortage of staff. Think of it as a version of your very own, in-house 'nowcasting' model, a forecasting method originally designed to analyse the weather but developed by leading industries to predict rapidly emerging economic trends. You choose the variables that will provide you with information likely to have the biggest impact. Like with a cash flow forecast, if you know three months beforehand that you are likely to be short of staff time, you will be able to do something about it. Being resilient is about reacting to change – the earlier you can see trouble brewing, the more likely you are to be able to fend it off.

Resource programming is also a critical part of forecasting your overall budget – multiplying each fee-earning staff member's total hours (remember, fee-earning staff can include non-architectural staff too – see Chapter 1) by their utilisation percentage and their charge out rate will show their basic fee turnover. To that figure must be applied a likelihood of fee recovery – not every invoice is paid, unfortunately (see 'Payment' in Chapter 5, page 85). If you were to add your practice overhead amount per year and distribute this evenly between your fee earners, you can then drill down into the numbers to see precisely what charge out rates should be applied to each member of staff. If you link their salary information to the calculation as well, you will see that even slight differences in charge out rates can affect their ability to deliver a profit.

This method also allows you to test the effect on your accounts of apportioning part or all of your own cost, if you are a practice director, to the business as an overhead. You can see from the variation in a director's utilisation percentage shown in Figure 2.2 that they are likely to consistently contribute the fewest productive, chargeable hours when compared to everyone else. Businesses like stability, so removing the director's contribution to the overhead means you can budget to use the other staff to cover that cost. This frees the director from the expectation of contributing a consistent daily number of hours to cover their portion of the overhead, because they themselves are accounted as an overhead. The result is that the boss has the flexibility to apply themselves to the problems of the day – matters which would otherwise take staff away from their programmed productive work hours. The added benefit to this arrangement is that any time which the director bills as chargeable is recorded as pure pre-tax profit,[3] because it is above the overhead allocation.

Remember, this is an accounting technique ultimately, and doesn't mean everything you touch turns immediately to gold, but it can influence the way in which you allocate resources when programming time for staff. In the example in the 'Resource allocation' box above, the architect was spending four to five hours a week on non-fee-earning work. Once you budget director time to things like visiting prospective jobs, dealing with unforeseen situations, briefing staff and reviewing invoices, you can find you're lucky if you manage to get four to five billable hours in a *week*. If this stings at first, remember it is better to know about it. You need to understand the figures, know how much you and your staff are worth and what they need to do to earn enough to cover costs and make a profit.

Once you know what time you have available from your workforce, you need to understand how much time each task will take. This is where your time sheets and job records play their part. Being disciplined about recording time against work stages and projects, tagging your projects as domestic, commercial, extension, conversion, new build and so on (see 'Sectors' on page 22), means you will be able to filter this information into categories. Being able to review past examples of work will help you to estimate how much time will be required for similar work not yet started. Time-recording software now available will help you find and sort this kind of information. The example above used Synergy, but there are plenty of alternatives available.

When deciding which software will be appropriate for your practice, consider how architects can spend long periods of time waiting for things to happen on a project – such as the granting of planning permission or the delivery of consultants' reports or surveys. During these periods, there is ongoing activity on the project, but perhaps barely enough to register on some time-recording systems, especially if they only measure time in days.

CASE STUDIES

Time sheets and resource planning

The following is a summary of responses from six different practices based severally in Leicester, Bristol, Bude, Manchester, London and Coventry and ranging in size from five employees to 85. They are all limited companies, with the oldest having been incorporated in 1979 and the most recent within the past five years.

A note of the full responses can be found in Appendix A, but Table 2.1 presents some key facts about the practices' time-recording activities.

Table 2.1: Time sheets

Number of people employed	What method is used for recording time?	What is the minimum time increment recorded?	Is time recorded separately for non-billable time?	Is the RIBA Plan of Work stage identified?
5	Spreadsheets	30 minutes	Yes	Yes
6	TimeSheet plugin integrated with Google Calendars	15 minutes	No, but total billable time is deducted from contracted hours weekly	Not in the time sheets, but is used in programme and progress reporting
12	Harvest	18 minutes	Yes	Yes
28	Deltek	15 minutes	Yes	Yes
65	CMap	15 minutes	Yes	Yes
85	CMap	15 minutes	Yes	Usually, unless project requires different approach

Every practice said their time sheets are used for invoicing purposes. There are other similarities, notably the minimum time increment of 15 minutes. Solicitors are known to charge out in six-minute increments; here, the trend clearly shows that a minimum increment of a quarter of an hour is adequate. Five of the six practices use dedicated software to record their time; this means they should have access to connected, digital analytics.

Table 2.2 summarises the practices' responses to questions specifically about planning resources.

Table 2.2: Resource planning

What software do you use to plan resources?	What do you call your office programme?	How far ahead do you plan resources?	How often do you review your office programme?
Spreadsheets	Deliverables Forecast	3 months	Weekly
Interlinked spreadsheets and online platform called briq.works	Project Pipeline	3 months	Weekly
Spreadsheets	Office programme	3 to 6 months, according to scale of project and scope of services	Weekly
Deltek	Project Pipeline	12 to 18 months	Monthly
CMap	Resource Plan	3 months	Fortnightly
CMap and spreadsheets	Resource Plan	3 months minimum	Weekly

It is noticeable, if unsurprising, that the three larger practices use their time-recording software to produce their variously titled 'resource plans', although one still uses spreadsheets alongside the reports available from CMap. Possibly, the software is more complex (and expensive) and enables more reporting to be taken from the data, or the larger practices can allocate more time to extracting data from the software, or a combination of both. Notwithstanding, when asked if their resource plans related to the time sheet data, all practices said they were not directly linked. They said there was a relationship, but it was either complementary, indirect or monitored on a project-by-project basis and manually cross-referenced.

The forward-planning period of three months ahead is consistent between practices, with the exception of the one that uses Deltek. This is less to do with the software and more to do with the type of projects which that practice works on: large residential blocks for universities, with long lead-in times and strict funding routines. Table 2.3 shows what other methods these practices use to analyse time-record data.

Table 2.3: Time-record analysis

Are time sheets filed under people or projects?	Do you compare actual time spent with time programmed?	Do you use time-record data to prepare fee proposals?	What else are your time records used for?
People, and collated manually if appropriate	Yes	Yes	Self-improvement
People, and shared through weekly meetings and reporting	Not often, but working towards this	Yes, especially larger projects, including assessment of brief against programme	Project management, and examining scope creep by using client design change trackers
Project, and each staff member enters their time onto a project record	Yes, using the software	Yes, especially larger projects; value of service delivered also reviewed	Monitoring efficiency (early warning at 80% of fee spend), informing future programmes and training
Project, and each staff member enters their time onto a project record	Yes, using WIP reports	Yes; projects are reviewed as they complete, and feedback informs future fee bids	Monitoring productivity and profitability
Project, and individual staff time-sheet reports can be produced if required	Yes, but it does not form part of staff performance reviews	Not so much	Monitoring projects, utilisation and profit and loss, and producing a range of KPIs; developing fee scale
Project, and individual staff time-sheet reports can be produced if required	Yes, but selectively for project audits	Yes	Monitoring projects, resourcing and profitability

It is interesting to uncover some of the ways that analysis of time records informs future fee bids. One of the case study practices (see the 'Case studies' box above) has used their own feedback to review future fee proposals for large projects in which they are to be part of a consortium. Current trends, such as the introduction of BIM and tighter planning rules on future design amendments, have shifted industry's expectations of what should now be included in detailed design information. The requirement is, in particular, for more up-front modelling and cost planning, which has forced this practice to reconsider the share of risk they are prepared to accept in project bids. Having examined the time spent in carrying out their work up to RIBA Stage 3, they could see that when they included the additional work they were now being expected to deliver up to the same stage, the percentages they had historically submitted in early negotiations would no longer cover even baseline costs. The additional work was seen to be as much as 10% more. Even should they be fortunate enough to make it to financial close, they have had to take a commercial view on their future risk share offers because the recovery of their risk is capped and does not include any win bonus.

Comments received from practices also described how, against the backdrop of changes in IT and the emergence of new tasks, the evaluation of working practices generally was leading to changes in methods of service delivery. Others reflected on what they can learn from examining their past performance on projects that might lead to them implementing self-evaluation or training, as well as considering how to improve specific activities, such as tightening up the briefing process applied at the outset as a way to limit the potential for scope creep and drifting programmes.

The last part of the RIBA Plan of Work is Stage 7. It is all about feedback, but is focused on post-occupancy reviews and the monitoring of building performance in use. Stage 6 is about the handover of the building, but it should also involve a 'Project Performance session' at which the project team can 'share their experiences for the benefits of future projects'.[4] This will help you to learn from your own performance in carrying out the project work, or to evaluate your own architectural services following completion of the project. It is increasingly common to hear the phrase 'lessons learned' – especially from politicians, following some incident or other – but actually learning from past mistakes to ensure they don't happen again requires a process. Looking back over activities undertaken on specific projects to see how they can be improved involves reflecting on why decisions were made to act or work in a particular way. For instance, did the initial project planning session lead to the right approach being used? If problems were encountered, were they the result of this or other factors? Were things done in a particular way simply because they have always been done that way or because it was right for that specific circumstance?

A successful evaluation process will start with agreeing a set of goals, such as what part of the service can be improved. A plan will then be formed to apply strategies to achieve those goals. It can be helpful to establish the goals by first asking the question '*What went well?*' and then finishing the sentence '*The project would have been even better if…*'. This process might lead to error-correction strategies being introduced, such as the implementation of a monitoring plan at the start of the next project. Such a plan might include a system for issuing prompts at critical moments during the work, for example, asking '*What do I need to know before I ...?*' or noting down what you did last time and predicting what might happen if you were to try something else. This builds in self-reflection and evaluation of actions during the project and demonstrates a method of applying 'lessons learned' from the outset, not just reviewing them on completion. This can lead to improvements in staff performance and skill, encouraging them to transfer what has been learned into new contexts, as well as potentially saving money in future projects by improving efficiency or reducing mistakes.

Endnotes

1 Architects Registration Board. *The Architects Code: Standards of Professional Conduct and Practice* (London: Architects Registration Board, 2017). Available at: https://arb.org.uk/architect-information/architects-code-standards-of-conduct-and-practice/ [accessed 18 January 2022].

2 Brian Pinder-Ayres, *Financial Management* (London: RIBA Publishing, 2016), p. 32.

3 If the director's pay is allocated as an overhead, any chargeable time invoiced is counted as profit. This arrangement is common among salaried directors, who also top up their pay with a regular dividend.

4 RIBA, *RIBA Plan of Work 2020 Overview* (London: RIBA, 2020), p. 64.

3

Providers

Threats to your business's survival can come at any time and from anywhere, so you need to take the basic mechanics of running a business seriously. No business will run by itself for long before some level of intervention is required, but expertise is available to help you. You will achieve better results if you accept you need to buy in the services of business experts, just as you would employ the services of a subconsultant on a design project, or to employ somebody with business expertise within the practice.

Obtaining money to help with your strategic plan for growth will lead you to the bank or some other lender. Assessing the benefit or otherwise of your investments is best done through interpretation of your accounts, but why not get more value from the services of your accountant. Collecting money owed to you is vital, but to give yourself more time to be an architect, how about employing others to collect it for you – they may even be better at it than you.

Architects understand that to protect their businesses against claims they need to purchase professional indemnity insurance. Indeed, this is a mandatory requirement of the profession. However, and possibly contrary to general thought, extracting the best value from your premium involves ensuring your broker gets to know you and your business. Other forms of insurance will protect you against other risks – separate from project work, but equally damaging. Employing staff, renting an office and operating a computer system can all put you at risk of being sued or having a claim made against you in addition to practising your profession.

The best form of defence against these risks is to know where they might come from and to prepare your business against them. While being resilient means being able to withstand shocks and bounce back from them, militating against potential impacts might make your business less likely to experience them at all.

Lender

While the role of the traditional bank manager figure has changed, due to computerisation and the emphasis on the sale of financial products,[1] banks still provide a critical lending function to businesses. This is fundamental to the economy. Even if the process has been quite dramatically depersonalised over the past 50 years or so, you still need to interact with someone somewhere to secure loans, overdraft facilities or other forms of borrowing. Focusing on building relationships with your lender is key.

Even though it may not be as straightforward as it once was to locate someone in a bank who you can talk to, most banks will provide account managers (or people with a similar title) who you can and should approach, even internet banks with no actual branches. (Internet banks may be slightly trickier to access, but consider whether a purely online bank can offer you what you need, remembering your business needs will change over time.) The moment you find you're looking for something other than simply a facility to make payments into and from, you might do worse than look around to find alternatives that offer some form of relationship manager.

When you approach a bank for money, either to invest or to provide you with a safety net (in the form of an overdraft), it is their job to assess you as a risk – how much they are prepared to give you is a matter of calculation, based on your company's financial profile and what you want the money for. Most high-street banks now host managers who make recommendations about lending decisions to a head office. The manager will need to justify the risk of accepting your business, usually through prerequisite application forms. There are other organisations, however, who pride themselves on their different culture and values. These so called 'relationship' banks will sometimes lend directly, where banks of the 'head office' model may not.

There are other ways to obtain money aside from the bank, of course. Banks can be a little pricey with set-up fees and charges, but they do offer you money for a wide range of reasons. Peer-to-peer lending is now more easily available, although the lenders may be more interested in lending for a specific activity and charges would still apply. Development funding can often be found from private investors willing to get involved in specific projects. Local investment groups are a good way to find out who may be interested in forming a single-project finance package, for instance, or may even offer some experience. If you are after money to buy another business (it's a quick way to grow your practice), there are several ways to raise this if the bank isn't willing, but acquisition funding is too complex to cover in this guide.

Whether it is a bank or another lending institution, there are no two ways about it: the bottom line is, whoever lends you the money will want it all back with interest. For a lender, you pose both a risk of losing money and an opportunity for making money. Their assessment of this simple calculation, coupled with your ability to demonstrate with certainty that you will pay back their money, is what will determine how much you will have to pay to borrow their money from them. You will need to assess how quickly you can pay it back and how much you can afford to pay in each instalment, because the cost of the borrowing will be pegged to these factors.

These variables will be different depending on the amount and the purpose of the loan. If it is money to pay for recruitment of a new member of staff, invest in some training, fund a marketing campaign, or all of these, you will need to pick a financial institution interested in lending money to you for these activities. If the money is for the purchase of products – new office furniture, for instance – you may be better off asking the supplier for an interest-free period for a specific term. This is the best form of borrowing as far as you are concerned, because you get what you wanted and you get to spread the cost over a fixed period of time, with a fixed outgoing each month, without it costing you more than if you made the purchase outright.

Stabilising your outgoings puts you in a better position to deal with uncertainty. Having fixed amounts to pay each month helps you set fee income targets and focuses the practice on meeting them each month. Short-term targets such as these can be tailored to incrementally improve the bigger picture when work is good by placing you in a position to set aside more profit. Alternatively, when work is slow coming in, or there is an unexpected financial threat to the business – perhaps through losing staff, a project being cancelled or an external threat – regular payment agreements should allow you an option to take a payment holiday by extending the terms of the loan. This can give you enough breathing space to enable a rescue plan to be actioned.

The best way to secure a loan is by having a carefully formulated business plan (and this will be essential whichever organisation you approach). If you are still at the stage of writing your plan, it can be helpful to seek advice about sources of financing. There is sometimes a benefit in using arenas outside the usual formal settings, such as local networking events or virtual forums. It can provide an opportunity for you to speak to individuals outside the walls of their institution. 'Budget breakfast' events hosted by accountancy practices or local chamber of commerce meetings can provide valuable opportunities for meeting other professionals. It might be easier for you to present yourself as capable, reliable and confident when both of you are off your own turf, and you may feel less vulnerable if you are not having to answer questions as they sit behind their computer screen.

The purpose of this approach is to build a network of alliances that you can draw upon to help your business. This applies not only when you have a new investment proposition, but also, and more critically, during those times when you face a financial threat. Increasing an overdraft or extending the terms of a loan is made easier if you have already set out your business plan or your 'relationship manager' already understands your business. Invariably, it is during turbulent times that decisions must be made quickly, in response to unwelcome circumstances. You will already be a step ahead if, during the calmer times, you have built relationships with your key providers.

Accountant

If your practice is a limited company, you will have to file accounts with Companies House and a tax return with HM Revenue and Customs, but even if you are a sole trader or a partnership, some form of accounts will be required in order to determine how much tax you need to pay. Most businesses use an accountant to prepare a set of trading records to determine their profitability for the previous 12 months. However, if you only see your accountant when they prepare these end-of-year (EoY) accounts for you, you should think about whether you could get more value from their services. There are things you have to do to run a business which are not covered in RIBA Parts 1, 2 or even 3 because they are not part of architecture, such as preparing trading accounts, invoicing and paying people (see 'Finance' and 'Payroll' below). Just as you would use a structural engineer to prepare calculations for long beams or retaining walls, or an ecologist to assess protected species' populations in buildings and sites, you should seek the expertise of financial professionals around you, especially for activities which will be repeated weekly, monthly or even annually for the rest of your career.

The EoY accounts give you an annual cross-sectional view of your practice. They summarise the state of health of the business at the same point in time each year – like an MOT or a health check. Interpretation of the profit and loss account and the balance sheet for the year will reveal shifts in performance compared with previous trading years. The preparation of EoY accounts allows you to see whether changes you have made over the course of the year have led to an improvement (or deterioration) in your business's overall financial performance. This point of reflection helps you to set goals and targets to focus on over the next year.

Management accounts are not EoY accounts. They tend not to focus on Corporation Tax (an annual payment), but they will include its accrual, along with payments for VAT (quarterly) and Income Tax (monthly). They give you summary snapshots of your business's current financial position at regular intervals through the year, usually monthly. The balance sheet is still based on past information, but, by being more regular than EoY accounts, these snapshots will enable swift analysis of any issues and problems, almost as they occur.

Management accounts show the total of all payments into and out of the business up to the point the EoY accounts are issued, so give you an accurate assessment of the money available for day-to-day use. This means they are essential for keeping track of cash flow. Management accounts include more detail about the breakdown of these totals than is contained in the EoY report. This means decisions on spending can be made quickly to ward off a specific, unscheduled risk, enabling corresponding decisions that will affect revenue – for instance, to alleviate a period of low income, it may be decided to temporarily shift resources to a particular project so that it reaches an invoice milestone more quickly, or, if that isn't quick enough, extend the use of an overdraft facility.

Income Tax now operates in a 'real time information' environment for Pay As You Earn (PAYE), and there is a move towards real-time accounting generally, likely resulting from being able to access financial figures so quickly using electronic accounting software. The benefit of this shift is that costs and liabilities traditionally only incorporated in the EoY report, such as depreciation, can now be reported continuously, resulting in a 'pay as you go' type culture. This puts in the hands of business leaders more accurate information about the actual state of their organisations than has previously been possible. However, the potential to take advantage of this with such immediacy could prove beguiling. Having too much access to information might become a distraction from the work itself – an image of the 'king in his counting house' comes to mind. Think of the frequency with which communications now reach us through messages, emails and social media; without introducing some degree of discipline, responding to all these calls for action can become the only business of the day – instead of carrying on with productive work. Be warned.

Your accountant can analyse a set of accounts as quickly as you can assess the potential of a site for a new development. They can also tell you about the trends and watchpoints the accounts reveal in just the same way as you are able to know when to bring in the expertise of a building services engineer rather than just stick a mechanical vent through the wall. Each of the component parts of your accounts tells a story of a part of your business. With interpretation these can help you understand the performance of your practice from different perspectives, and enable you to make better informed decisions about how and where you go next. I have already talked about the calculation of working capital, your trading position and percentages of productive work, which can feed into several aspects of the way you might run your business. Instead of limiting the interaction with your accountant to once a year and concentrating on historical figures, you could plan more regular meetings to review and discuss the monthly or quarterly results and to consider subtle changes (or even bold ones) to your plans for the business.

Regular meetings with your accountant need last no more than an hour or so, and if your accounts are kept using online software you should be able to produce balance sheets, profit and loss accounts and work in progress lists for each week, month or quarter as you need them (although regular profit and loss accounts might not always produce flattering numbers). Alternatively, your accountant can log in to your accounts and directly review the reports necessary for the meeting. Holding meetings like these means the preparation of your EoY accounts will be simpler too, because you may be able to agree certain cost offsets or allocations for activities such as office repairs or improvements during the year. This means the EoY accounts are essentially a summary of the reports prepared for the meetings held throughout the year.

At these meetings, you should consider budget setting, charge out rates, hire purchase agreements, future salaries, bonuses and tax burdens. For instance, setting up and examining budgeting for salaries (almost like a cash flow forecast) will be useful if you need to quickly consider the true costs of employing more staff and comparing them with the improved returns. You can also review the way your own costs are attributed, whether as a straight salary that contributes an equal proportion to the business overheads or as a full overhead (see 'Resourcing' in Chapter 2, page 33). Apportioning some or all of your cost as principal as an overhead leaves you free to win work, run the business or train people without worrying about losing fee-earning time. You might test fluctuations of the amount of fee-earning time which suits you (and the business) over the course of a year.

Your annual costs can be categorised into groups, which can be made up in a way that suits the set-up of your practice. You might consider adopting the groupings used in the mandatory annual RIBA Business Benchmarking survey, for instance, which collates all premises costs into one category, including rent, lighting, heating and cleaning. Alternatively, you may prefer to group all non-architect salaries together, including (if you have one) a cleaner, alongside support staff, so you can easily see the amount you are spending on people who are not fee earners, or to split off the value that non-architectural staff will add to your fee income (see 'Profile' in Chapter 1). You can use any groupings that will help you to make decisions. Note, however, that there should be a good reason for changing these groupings, because annual comparisons of figures (at year end) will be more useful and informative if they are on a like-for-like basis. The point here is simply that you can work out how to track your trading position by capitalising on the expertise of the other professionals around your business.

Apart from anything else, running a business is hard work, but it can be made a bit easier by having an accountant on hand who knows your business and who you can turn to for advice. Just as you must have sat in front of clients who thrash out their domestic priorities when preparing a brief for their new house, making you feel more like a counsellor (or a dispute resolution expert) than an architect, you should sometimes take advantage of being able to do the same. None of us are made of iron and we all need a sounding board from time to time. Running a small practice means you are less likely to have a board of directors, or even another co-director, to bounce new ideas off or test alternative ways of doing things. Often it will be just you, but that doesn't mean you have to do it all on your own – you can and should ask those people you place around you to help.

Finance

Sending out invoices is one of the most important tasks when running a business. Without invoices, you will simply have no money coming in and your survival is doomed. This is obvious to just about everyone, and yet in architecture practices invoicing is not always treated with the level of importance it deserves. It must happen regularly and accurately, and be followed up rigorously to ensure every invoice is paid.

If you take a moment to pace out the time between doing work and receiving money for that work, you will recognise the vital importance of operating a cash flow forecast to control the balance of money coming in and going out. An overdraft should be used to cover the inevitable, but hopefully infrequent, moments when the two don't balance. Having a forecast should limit these occasions to very few. If they become more frequent, you should think about taking action to correct the imbalance. Overdrafts should be thought of as a way to ease unexpected pressure on cash flow, but if they become anything other than that, a different form of long-term finance will be cheaper.

If you operate a business – with all the work that entails – and you still expect personally to be able to give invoicing the time and attention it needs, good luck to you. However, you should consider the following:

- Is invoicing really the best use of your time?
- Do you have the correct skills for this task?

Employing someone to prepare invoices makes sense – it saves you time and ultimately pays for itself. Your chances of getting paid are increased if invoices are issued by someone from a finance role or department, rather than by you.

For a client, being confronted with a separation of these roles might help them, as they may respond differently to you and to another person in your office. With you, their architect, they have built a detailed relationship centred on complex design solutions and resolving problems, involving frustrations and deliberations on both sides. In other words, they expect a bit of arm-wrestling. If they take the same approach to any queries on your invoice, and apply the same set of behaviours, payment of the invoice can become more troublesome than it need be. But if the client has to take up a payment query with someone else, whose sole aim is to collect money for the business, another, simpler set of expectations are brought into play. The results can be better for cash flow and the maintenance of good relationships. (See also 'Payment' in Chapter 5, page 85.)

PRACTICE INSIGHTS

Invoicing

From my own experience, I know I will spend longer than I should on preparing each invoice I intend to issue – on trying to get the tone right, as well as the timing and the amount. I also know this is unlikely to make the slightest difference to whether a client is going to pay me. Yet even writing that sentence slightly chills me, because I still carry a vestige of belief that my intervention will make the difference – but no, no it won't. It is simply not the case.

I don't know of any other group of professionals that makes such a meal out of issuing invoices for work they have done (except perhaps actors and artists – clearly, it is the creative types who have the most trouble recognising the true value of their craft). To eliminate this costly deliberation, invoicing should be carried out by someone else – somebody who can simply measure the time it took to create the work and then process the sum due accordingly.

The financial activities you are likely to encounter in running a business also deserve the time and skills that specialists can bring to them. As well as the preparation of invoices, tasks related to purchase orders, payment of bills, subscriptions, loan interest, bank reconciliation and cash flow forecasts, as well as calculation of VAT, can all be undertaken by someone other than you. Readily available accounting software can be a powerful tool for your practice, but, while much of it is simple to use, ultimately it requires information to be inputted regularly for it to provide you with the full spread of its features. The right person using some straightforward accounting software would be able to prepare your regular management accounts, giving you more time to review and analyse the immediate trends.

Apart from the obvious benefits of freeing up time for you to use in running your business, the addition of a member of staff capable of performing these tasks provides you with in-house expertise on money matters. There are multiple ways of reporting financial information and regular reports from software can tell you much, but the scope and interpretation of such reports is what really counts. Reviewing important matters, such as budget setting, charge out rates, bonus payments or purchase options for new equipment, all require careful thought and analysis. Putting people around you who understand your business's financial information is not only helpful, but can also provide challenge, justification and confidence for making decisions.

Payroll

Always remember that your staff must be paid for their work accurately and on time (see also 'Needs' in Chapter 4, page 64). Organising the payment of salaries is the primary function of a payroll department. You can try and do this yourself, but, as in the other areas covered in this chapter, there is value in hiring an expert to do it. There are two main drawbacks to doing this work yourself. The first is the time it takes – time you should be spending doing architecture. This carries the double cost of preventing you getting through your programmed work and stopping you earning fees. The second is the risk of getting things wrong – mistakes could take up even more time and could be expensive in a number of ways, such as through the costs of tribunals, compensation, repayments and losing staff.

The confidential nature of a person's salary can raise issues about the security of information if wages are calculated and distributed within the office, although this is not a reason on its own to hire someone specifically to manage your payroll. Workers' salaries are calculated according to their individual circumstances, and people are not all the same. Qualified staff may need to have student loan payments deducted. If you employ at least one person, you must put certain staff into a workplace pension scheme and make contributions to it (see the Pensions Act 2008). Tax deductions will vary, and sick pay, maternity leave and holidays all bring additional layers of complexity. During the coronavirus pandemic, the government made furlough payments for some workers, which came with strict controls and criteria.

In preparing Income Tax payments, a perplexing array of 'P' forms are required to record the firm's payments to yourself and staff, from P11D (to calculate any benefits in kind you have enjoyed) to P32 (summarising the specific payments made to HMRC each month) and P60 (recording the annual total paid for each individual on your books); not to mention P45 for new starters, and a Starter Checklist for those who don't have a P45!

These layers of complexity may lead you to conclude that there is value in employing a separate payroll department or subscribing to an online service provider, depending on the scale of your operations. Such an arrangement can also provide additional value. Someone whose skills and expertise are centred around the calculation and payment of salaries can offer advice on appropriate salaries for different grades, pay rises, procedures relating to time off for sickness, maternity or paternity, and so on. You could think of them as the 'quantity surveyors of salary' – the analogy is that you can probably estimate a budget price for some building work using a square metre rate, a friendly builder can offer you an estimate for an extension to a domestic property, but only a quantity surveyor can calculate the precise cost, using a schedule of the materials and work involved, an index for when the work is due to start and the correct contingency to be applied.

Payroll services will often provide human resources (HR) services too. Employment contracts will need to set out working hours, a job description and holiday entitlements, and also grievance and disciplinary procedures. Off-the-shelf contracts are available; however, you might wish to include more specific details and an HR expert can help with this. A contract of employment can provide your business with some degree of flexibility and protection against a sudden downturn in work. When your resource programme shows you may not have enough work to keep all your staff busy, you might risk losing good workers only to find that an influx of work follows shortly afterwards. A short-time working clause in your staff employment contracts can help you avoid losing staff by allowing a flexible approach to dealing with those times when there is not enough work to go around. But for this to work needs you to be open with staff at the beginning – when you become aware of the potential for a drop-off in project work – so that everyone understands the situation you are all about to face. You may be surprised at how understanding and practical your staff can turn out to be when this happens. This kind of policy will help the business ride out risks from a shortage of work and can make for a stronger bond between staff when it is over. Setting up these contract terms with staff might be easier if you have the help of someone with the necessary expertise.

Insurance broker

This section is not about professional indemnity insurance – you have to skip to the next section for that. Rather, it is about the myriad other insurances available to you, some of which you need and others you might think are nice to have.

If your practice employs anyone, you must have employers' liability insurance. For each day you don't have insurance, the government can fine you £2,500, and your policy must cover you for at least £5 million. It is essentially health and safety insurance to protect you and your staff if someone is injured at work, but it can also provide cover to employers against the risk of a tribunal if serious injury has been caused. For an employee of an architecture practice, the place of work will most likely include construction sites in various stages of completion and in different locations; your policy will need to include such risky locations. Some policies will come with advice on human resource issues too.

In addition to protecting you and your staff, you must consider insurance that covers members of the public who visit you in the office (public liability insurance), as well as protecting your office itself and its contents against risks of fire and theft (buildings and contents insurance).

With the acceptance of electronic project records in lieu of hard copies and the introduction of the General Data Protection Regulation, storage of data has become a potential risk. Cyber crime is not just targeted at giant businesses; many small firms have been affected, suffering extortion threats demanding payouts in Bitcoin. If any breach of office data occurs, it must first be reported to the Information Commissioner's Office, but then swiftly dealt with. Cyber risk insurance policies not only provide protection against losses caused by such events, but can also provide critical advice at the point when you need it most – essentially helping you to deal with a security breach. Selecting the right cyber risk policy – one that include these services – takes time, so is perhaps a task best given to someone who knows about such things.

The cyber cover is designed to protect you from potentially substantial losses and the threat of being unable to continue to trade. Incidents that result in lost time or data can be more damaging than the theft of a computer. With more and more work being stored digitally, losing access to that data means your work continuity is severed. Everyone has suffered the pain of a corrupted file and had to reluctantly accept it is quicker to recreate what has been lost, but if this is multiplied over an office's entire portfolio, you might lose your stock-in-trade overnight. Cyber risk policies often include an obligation to install back-ups, to prevent you from ever reaching that position – this can be a good moment to focus on ensuring you have a system in place.

Other types of policy you may wish to consider, depending on your circumstances, include sick pay insurance and key worker insurance. Being able to offer enhanced sick pay insurance might prove the difference in your next recruitment drive – it may mean you are able to offer better employment terms and conditions than a rival practice, which is also keen to land the newest and brightest talent in the jobs market.

Key worker insurance may be essential to the firm, as it would guarantee you can maintain a minimum monthly income should your lead architect or director, or other key member of staff, become sick and incapable of working for a period of time. The loss to the business would be twofold, as the member of staff would not be able to do the work required and the practice would need to employ someone to replace them. An architecture practice does not enjoy the benefit of being able to call on locum staff, as a hospital or school could.

Two small practices operating in the same area may choose to set up an informal arrangement, so that one would help the other if either were to lose a key worker, which can be reassuring. A good starting point for this arrangement would be to conduct a first meeting at which each practice introduces its office systems and structures to the other. Subsequently, there would only need to be an annual meeting, to review the type of projects on the books. Sole traders are particularly vulnerable, and when small practices reach out to offer this level of safety net it can build positive relationships between fellow professionals. This can lead to other shared activities, such as CPD and social events. Some local RIBA branches may already facilitate this.

Buying business insurance is not like buying private car insurance from a comparison website. Deciding which policy will benefit you requires expertise, so it really is worthwhile obtaining business insurance through a broker. The broker you use may be different to your professional indemnity insurance broker, but they need not be. The right broker will be able to advise you on the most suitable protection for your circumstances and can be helpful in the event of a potential claim. Think how your clients come to you because of your knowledge – you should do the same when it comes to running your business. Ultimately, it will save you time and provide you with better protection.

Professional indemnity insurance

Professional indemnity insurance (PII) is mandatory for practising architects. For any issues relating to PII, your insurance broker is your first point of contact, but they are not the ones actually insuring you. Your broker has professional relationships with insurers, who are the firms that underwrite your trading risks. The broker will first assess your business and your insurance needs, and then search the insurance market to find an insurer who can provide appropriate cover for you. Your policy is with the 'insurer' and you are the 'insured', and in the same way that you act as contract administrator on a building contract – managing the relationship between the employer and the contractor – your broker administrates the relationship between you and the insurer. They know insurance the same way you know construction.

If you don't know your PII broker by name, they don't know you, and that could be a problem because it means they won't necessarily know how you protect your practice against being sued. If you think your premium will go up just because you report an incident to them, you need to discuss this with them directly, because the likelihood is it won't. Even the simplest of matters can result in administration costs, and sometimes solicitor's fees, but, unless the number of alerts become considerable, alerting your insurer with precautionary notifications won't increase your premium.

> Insurers definitely value good risk management and proof of this when negotiating renewal terms can be very beneficial.
>
> Nicky Francis, Director, ASE Insurance Agency (UK) Ltd

Brokers are in the business of assessing risk, but the insurance companies they broker for take this to the next level. To the insurer, how you protect yourself has a direct relationship with how you protect them against a payout. If you experience an incident that results in your insurer being involved, they will want to know what you have done to mitigate the risk of them having to pay out. The benefit of building a working relationship with your broker is that they can be an effective bridge between you and the insurer. But to be able to communicate clearly and accurately with the insurer, your broker needs to understand the way your firm operates and manages its risk.

Within your policy, there will be an obligation on you to let your insurer know as early as possible of any circumstances that might lead to a claim against your policy. It might be worded as follows:

> If the Insured shall become aware during the Period of Insurance of any Circumstance the Insured shall as a condition precedent to the right to be indemnified under this policy give notice as soon as practicable to the entity at Section 11 of the Schedule during the Period of Insurance or within 14 days after the expiry of the Period of Insurance.
>
> For the avoidance of doubt, notice under this policy is not valid if given by any third party (other than the Insured's insurance agent on the Insured's instructions).

The policy wording allows you to pass that information to the insurer via your broker ('the Insured's insurance agent'). Going through your broker can be invaluable, as it allows the broker to use their expertise and experience to make their own assessment of the risk you may be exposed to. It will also ensure that you provide sufficient information for the insurer to make their own assessment. If this seems a little hierarchical or convoluted, don't think about it that way. Instead, consider the value of you broker's experience in such matters and benefit from it.

The more your broker knows about how you operate, the more advice they can offer to help you prevent matters from escalating. In the event of an allegation, it is highly likely you will be faced with having to speak to the person making the allegation against you before you have received specific advice from your insurer. In these circumstances, your broker can guide you in the appropriate action to take, such as sending a holding email containing specific, non-prejudicial wording to cover the period when you are waiting for the insurer's viewpoint. This helps protect you in two ways: first, the advice will be relevant to the specific situation you are facing; and, second, as your insurer has allowed you to discuss matters with your broker, they will be less likely to view your actions as out of turn.

You have to be alert to any situation that could result in an allegation against you. It might simply be something a contractor said casually when you were on site, or a client muttered when they were on the phone – something that chimed with you just enough to make you suspect not everything was running smoothly. The onus is on you to write it down and get it over to your broker for them to consider, or at the very least be alert to – you can always follow up with more detailed information after raising the alarm. After reviewing the matter, if your broker says it's nothing to worry about, then you can relax. Remember, the onus on you is to report a 'circumstance' likely to give rise to a claim, you shouldn't simply wait for an allegation.

When you do report an issue, be searingly honest – you need to be able to assess your own performance in the situation. If you don't tell your broker everything, they have less chance of being able to help you and it might invalidate your indemnity later. If your broker doesn't want you to report everything, get a new broker and a new deal. They need to know what you are doing to reduce risk. See Appendix B for more detail on writing to report an issue to your insurer.

Endnotes

1 There are obviously myriad reasons why banks have changed significantly since the 1960s, including political factors, regulation and deregulation, rising wages, a new consumer society and credit cards etc. For simplicity, only two prominent reasons are considered here.

Part 2

People

4

Staff

Your staff are your most valuable resource. But are they satisfied with what they are being asked to do? Are they happy with the environment in which they work? Do you pay them enough attention? If the answer to any of these questions is 'no', you can quickly find yourself losing time and money, and possibly much more. You could lose their skills and their potential expertise you have not yet tapped into. Consider the different ways to ensure you take care of your staff, particularly by including them in the decisions you need to make and by investing in them and their needs.

In business, you will mostly make decisions about the here and now, but there is an alternative time scale. This relates to those decisions you make which may not result in anything for some considerable time. However, after putting something in place for the future, it will start taking shape before you know it. This type of investment is of particular value when applied to staff; committing to improve staff skills over a period of time is like sowing seeds. It enriches the day-to-day when suddenly something new happens.

If the vision for your practice focuses on growth, your strategic plan will have to support this ambition. This could lead you to adopt a tailored recruitment policy – one that includes targeting specific skill sets you either don't have or do, but wish to expand, increasing the number of staff of a certain grade to manage a new working arrangement, or even implementing a training programme to address gaps in knowledge that are easy to fill from within the practice. To make your business more resilient you need to carry out a straightforward analysis of your practice and respond to what you find.

Improving the diversity of your workforce and creating an environment in which people feel valued, where they have opportunities to grow professionally and can gain satisfaction from the work they are doing on a day-to-day basis, will result in a resilient workforce. Improving working conditions will help make the practice flexible enough to respond to a changing world, and can generate longer-term benefits through improved practice reputation, financial resilience (as you won't have to keep recruiting new staff) and adaptability (to new ways of working). The common purpose is to make the business successful – which benefits everyone; by creating a team, you will engender an atmosphere of trust, where each member looks out for the others.

Transparency

It pays to share your aims and intentions for the practice with your staff. How else can they help you achieve them? This means opening up about the good and bad bits. The earlier part of this guide notes the importance of creating a culture of resilience among your staff and of establishing a shared vision. It is obvious to see why this vision needs to be agreed by everyone, but what information and decisions should you share? The answer is a reflection perhaps of how much you trust your staff. As a leader, you need to establish the rules within the organisation and model the behaviour you expect. Sharing information or decision-making with your staff can encourage contributions you might not expect. It is also helpful for understanding the potential in people and learning what they care about – what they say can reveal a lot about them.

Engaging a social media company to take over the responsibility of posting information about the practice's work, activities and successes, or even starting a conversation internally about how to present the practice online, can be a positive way to encourage transparency. It might start with a round table discussion about what content everyone wishes to share on the internet about the company and themselves. This will highlight the connection staff feel with the company by revealing what they want said about where they work, as well as what they themselves want to say. In a way that has not previously been possible, a worker's personal life – through their social media accounts – and the company they work for have become 'linked', quite literally, by setting up connections, or liking and sharing, between accounts. This is a two-way street – what they say might not be what you would say – and there needs to be a protocol or agreement about what is acceptable and what is not.

Other opportunities for transparency include discussions about what new projects the practice should take on, what fees have been spent on specific projects or what gains or losses have occurred on others. When sensitively handled, this can help to bind a group of people around a common purpose and create a team.

Open conversations about fees with staff – where a project is succeeding or failing – shouldn't just happen in private with the project lead; these situations affect everyone in the business, and they matter. By being brought into the open, a discussion can reveal how or where other staff can help. In 'Fee earners' in Chapter 1, the terms and ratio of fee earners to non-fee earners was discussed. Non-fee earners traditionally provide support and back-up, which can be crucial in freeing up time, creating space or simply making a staff member feel supported, practically and emotionally, when they have to get through a tough patch. Non-fee-earning staff should also be considered an equal part of the team and made to realise that their contributions are relevant too – because they are. It is easier to call on colleagues to help you get through tight spots if they have a general understanding of the state of the practice's various projects and general workload. (See 'Payment' in Chapter 5, page 85, for a specific way this can help.) If conversations like these are made part of everyday communication, they will become less precious. Anything that can be discussed should be discussed.

Training

Training should be considered in relation to each individual member of staff's needs as well as to how it ties into the firm's strategic plan. It should not be limited to professional staff and their mandatory continuing professional development (CPD) nor generally aimed solely towards fee-earning staff. A training programme should capitalise on the potential strengths of all staff members, including those who are non-fee earning. Annual or periodic reviews provide you with the opportunity to suggest to staff areas where you feel they are low in skills and may need some support, but they are also a good way to raise the prospect of other training or development opportunities. The following box suggests some options to consider when planning to implement a comprehensive staff training plan.

TRAINING PROGRAMME

Achieving goals

You should be able to demonstrate how a programme of investment in training will improve the chances of the practice achieving the goals stated in the strategic plan and meeting your business aims. Perhaps you have committed to improving 3D drawings or have decided to offer a budget-costing service to your clients – courses can be targeted directly to meet these ambitions.

Core CPD

All professional staff must undertake a mandatory programme of CPD – such as the RIBA core series. However, each individual's programme can be supplemented by other sources of training, over a cycle of, say, three to five years, to keep the training varied. Keeping a record of the courses attended by each staff member can help you to identify which of the sessions on offer will provide them with a rounded curriculum. To help stretch resources, structured CPD can be supplemented with lunchtime seminars, online product webinars and informal reading.

Inclusion

Look at the core CPD available and consider showing the list to non-architectural staff – such as administration staff – so they can choose a topic of particular interest to them. Many of the topics on offer could provide them with a positive understanding of the project-related activities the architectural staff work on. This 'cross-pollination' opens up opportunities for better support between staff and can also unlock a passion and interest to learn more.

Academic learning

Often, local government organisations or education and training networks will link up with colleges to offer learning at reduced rates to businesses within their catchment area. These might include short courses in subjects such as marketing, management or public speaking. They can lead to academic qualifications level 2, 3, 4 or, even, 5.[1] A staff member who enrols as a student might require some time off for study – half to one day a week for a six- to eight-week course – or space may be required for an assessment to be carried out in the office. Offering all staff the option to sign up to one of these courses, when the opportunity arises, can bring surprising results. It can initiate a spark in someone who may not have shown an interest in anything like that before – building the capacity of your staff yields rewards.

Learning and education should be seen as life-long activities, and encouraging all workers in your business to engage in some form of improvement is the greatest investment you can make.

These improvements can be measured against targets or key performance indicators (KPIs) to assess the impact the training is having. If the overarching business goal is improvement, this can be broken down into different areas; targets or KPIs can then be set for these areas to allow improvements to be measured. Usually, the initial results will show that targets are set too high or too low, or you have too many or too few of them to be of value, but after a short trial period, they can become very powerful tools.

During the 2020 coronavirus lockdown, one practice noticed improved business results as a direct result of increasing the amount they spent on their training programme (see the box below). The programme usually included a plan to help staff get more out of existing software, but the practice switched their attention to training centred around the person and their personality. Starting in the boardroom and gradually moving to the associate directors, they experienced 'transformational results'. From an initial assessment process backed up with mentoring, the improvements in areas such as self-awareness were so effective they have now rolled out this training to all staff.

PRACTICE INSIGHTS

Personal development training

By Gavin Sorby, Managing Director, Buttress Architects Ltd, Manchester

During the 2020 lockdown, the board went through an alternative training course centred on the individual skills of each person and their personality. The board felt the benefits of this process were such that all staff members should go through it. We have now concluded that process. The greatest benefits were improved self-awareness and an understanding that we all perceive and react to situations differently. Each person is unique and every individual gets something different from the process – something that is relevant to them.

The training identifies strengths, and also areas where an individual may not be as strong. There is no right or wrong, just different. Our studio needs 'different' – nobody can be brilliant at everything. We all have blind spots; identifying, understanding, being comfortable with and playing to individuals' strengths across the studio is very powerful. Equally powerful is understanding and being able to say 'just be aware, I'm not great at that' to set an expectation, rather than creating stress for the individual concerned and a poor outcome.

We are now looking at ways to include shorthand summary profiles of all our staff on our intranet, so we all know what to expect of each other and appreciate how best to interact to get the best results. We have also started to look at the mix of strengths we have at board level and how that might change with succession, and similarly for teams within the studio.

Needs

All staff members experience pressure at times, so you should look for innovative ways to address those pressures and consider what your staff might need. This is not only about the pressures they experience in work, but external pressures too. Pressures on staff from home, family and day-to-day 'life admin' play a key role in the efficiency and performance of the business. Pay attention and be generous. Architecture can be a high-pressure environment – there is usually a lot of money at stake and risks can be significant. At the same time, though, it's not life and death.

Never forget, people work for money. If you are running your own business, it can be easy to become frustrated when your employees don't seem to put the same effort into their work that you do. If you reach this point, you have forgotten that they work for money. It is your responsibility to create an environment that can provide them with more than this, a place where they are valued and can grow as individuals.

In March 2020, when the first national lockdown was imposed during the coronavirus pandemic, flexibility in the workplace gained an importance it had never had before. From that date, working from home became normal for almost everyone who was lucky enough to be in work and for whom working from home was possible. However, a pandemic should not be the only reason for having a policy on working from home or flexible working.

There is almost nothing requiring greater clarity than the issue of time off work. Staff need time off for multiple reasons, including: illness, child's or parent's illness, bereavement, maternity or paternity leave, emergencies (e.g. house or car repairs), training, bank holidays and annual leave. There are plenty of other reasons, and only some of them can be planned for. How you respond as an employer to requests for time off can make a difference to the health and wellbeing of your staff, as well as to their performance. You need a policy to help you respond when faced with a request for time off, in just the same way as your staff need to know where they stand when they need to ask for it.

PRACTICE INSIGHTS

Agile working policy

We introduced an agile working policy in 2018 designed to provide each member of staff with opportunities to find a balance between the time they are in work and the time they are not. It is based around an agreed range of core working hours and expectations, allowing individual members of staff to consider how their needs are best met. It was designed to be responsive to people's needs at the time, but was not a change to their contract of employment. The policy is reproduced in Appendix C.

Fairness

All members of staff deserve to be treated equally, which includes making demands of them and meeting their needs fairly. Now, stop to consider whether your staff are being treated equitably. Can you say you are providing every member of staff with the same opportunity in the workplace? Establishing a culture in which everyone feels they are being given a fair opportunity creates a positive and inclusive work environment, which helps businesses to respond to change and recognise potential in people.

Ensuring all your staff have the same chances to fulfil their potential creates a better environment in which to work. This will make people enjoy working in your business more and, when considered jointly with an agile working policy (see 'Needs' above), you have the opportunity to build fairness into your staff offer, which will help you to attract and retain the best talent.

PRACTICE INSIGHTS

Fairness

By Marsha Ramroop, Director of Inclusion and Diversity, RIBA

Being fair in the workplace requires understanding that what you might think is fair, someone else may not. That doesn't mean either of you are right or wrong, you just have different perspectives. Coming to an agreement when perspectives are different requires emotional intelligence and cultural intelligence. Developing these skills is core to being inclusive, especially because we are all inherently biased,[2,3] and it's a fallacy that by simply knowing we're biased we can mitigate it.[4] So, we need to create procedural changes to mitigate the impact of hidden bias. This means having clear, objective hiring procedures; making progression steps and opportunities available to all staff; conducting independent exit interviews and acting on feedback, etc. Taking the time to do this work well pays dividends, ethically as well as financially.

The Equality Act 2010 replaced three earlier pieces of legislation and applies to all employers. Most architects are familiar with the Act through the Building Regulations Approved Document M: *Access to and use of buildings*, and will be aware of what it means for them as employers running a business. It applies equally to how services are provided to clients and the way staff are treated. The Act aims to ensure that staff are treated fairly by employers, and it refers explicitly to pay and recruitment.

When recruiting, you should be aware that you are permitted to apply what is known as 'positive action'. If you have two candidates of equal standing, you are entitled to take positive action to select the one who will improve the diversity in your business.[5] Construction has traditionally been a male-dominated environment – positive action is one way to make the sector more gender equal.

Introducing a diversity and inclusion strategy to your business planning will result in a diverse workforce, one that includes people of all genders, sexuality, races and dis/abilities. This makes it more likely you will attract a more diverse range of talent too, which will bring more varied opinions, different backgrounds and life experiences, as well as new perspectives on ways of working. It can also open new markets – being able to show you are an inclusive workplace may make you more attractive to client groups you have not previously worked for.

> Diversity is about recognising the value of difference.
> Inclusion is about ensuring we get the best from everyone.[6]

There are long-term business benefits to organisations that include policies aimed to make them more representative of society. The coronavirus pandemic introduced hybrid working arrangements, which previously would have been the exception but are now not uncommon. With flexible working hours becoming generally accepted, staff who have young families may be able to stay in work for longer or be supported in returning to work after a break (especially women). It will also allow others to re-evaluate their career choices, such as those who have elderly parents or relatives who require more care.

Just as providing ramps allows everyone, not just wheelchair users, to get into buildings, policies built on fairness and equality of opportunity make businesses more relevant to the wider economically active population. Being able to demonstrate credibility requires evidence of these values in all aspects of your practice. Encouraging respect and openness, making a workplace free of bias, recruiting from diverse backgrounds, publicly stating your ambition, communicating through marketing your commitment to the journey to embed equality, diversity and inclusion into your business are ways to show this. This may present you with many challenges, but it is a question of outlook – if your business model reflects society, your service offer will appeal to a wider audience.

Communication

If you are a leader, the number of opportunities staff have to talk to you or raise something with you may be fewer than you think. Being in a small office does not mean anyone can or will say anything that is on their mind at any time, because they don't. And for people working from home or working part-time, their chances of catching you to discuss something may be fewer still. You have to make room for these conversations.

Being in charge means there are many competing demands on your time, and you must allocate sufficient time to every one of them. I heard about a seminar on running your own business at which the speaker challenged his audience with a question: 'How do you get three holidays every year?' The audience looked expectantly at him ... 'Book 'em!', he said, triumphantly. He was dead right, and finding space in the day for opportunities to talk with staff will only happen if you 'book 'em' – just like holidays.

Although it can sometimes seem as if all you do each day is attend meetings, the people you are meeting with may not feel the same way, particularly your staff. When they have an issue they need to discuss with you, it is their chance to talk to you as well. Whether they want to get something off their chest or get you to resolve something that is preventing them from making progress, these opportunities should not be seen by you as just another meeting. As mentioned in 'Time recording' in Chapter 2, it may help you to appreciate the value of the time you spend on various management activities if you record non-fee-earning time in different categories. When you look back over a week and see how much time you actually spent on non-project work, it may be less than you initially imagined. You can create as many different categories in your time sheet 'house accounts' as you want, but if you try to relate them specifically to how you will budget your time over the year, they will become more useful to you if they can be grouped together. This way, you can make an assessment of the value each activity provides to your business and apportion your available time accordingly.

Notwithstanding the above, it could equally be the case that staff will comment on the number of meetings they are required to attend, which might prevent them from finishing what they are working on within the allocated time available to them. However, it is far better that a staff member has to postpone or cancel a meeting than that they are never given an opportunity to talk to you.

Consider the many reasons why you might need to talk with staff. The simple day-to-day office matters could include: programme, projects, administration,

> **PRACTICE INSIGHTS**
>
> **Making time for conversations**
>
> Early in the global coronavirus pandemic, in March 2020, we set up a 9 am briefing on Zoom for all staff – every working day of the week. After a month or so there were some suggestions we could reduce the frequency of briefings. It was said that other practices were meeting only once a week, or only required staff to phone in to their line-manager when they had any problems. We discussed reducing the frequency, but there was no consensus so we stuck with the format. By the end of the summer of that year, we were, like most offices, blending home working with some office work, and we were never all in the same place at the same time. The frequency of our morning briefings was discussed again, and this time it was agreed – by everyone – that keeping the daily 9 am format was the best thing we could have done. For staff members, the simple regularity of the briefings – being able to see everyone else every morning – meant they knew they would always have an opportunity to raise a pressing issue.

changes in systems and structures, procedures, diary management, advice or assistance, etc. But what about when someone has health issues, or their dog needs to go to the vet, or they are struggling and might need some help with something, or even need time off? All of these affect the way someone can work. Paying attention to such issues is not only compassionate, but good for the business. Like any other team, when one person is off their game, goals can be missed. It doesn't all have to come from you, however; by uniting transparency, delegation and trust in all staff, and communicating with each other regularly, everyone has a part to play.

When matters do arise, deal with them straight away – especially the tricky ones. If you begin to think, even momentarily, there may be something more going on in a situation, there probably is. You should trust your instinct. If you already have regular meetings scheduled in, such as briefings or project reviews, and it can wait until then, raise the issue there and see if it can be resolved quickly. If not, make an exception, set aside time that day to discuss your concerns with the people involved.

Having this kind of conversation with staff is not easy – for them or you. It will be helpful to you if you plan the sequence of events before the meeting starts and then follow a clear structure, such as:

listen → agree action → implement

There are lots of alternative methods, but one helpful structure from education, known as STORM,[7] is summarised below:

State the issue: You start, clearly setting out what you are concerned about and what positive outcome you want.

Their side: Let them respond with their views while you listen.

Options: Jointly consider what can be done, but don't commit to a solution.

Resolution: Let them propose what they will do to remedy the issue and agree when.

Move on: Leave the issues in the meeting, acknowledge the positives and agree a date to review.

Lastly, a word on briefing or imparting information. No matter how many times you think you've made something clear, make it clearer – say it again, write it, email it. Just as we all see things differently, we all hear things differently too. As architects, we all know this. When a builder asks you a question on site, once you've answered, try asking them to tell you what you just said – they rarely can.

Ambition

Building capacity in people does not always have to be targeted towards the tasks or activities they are paid to undertake – it can and should be wider than that. Do you know what your staff want to achieve? Do you know what their outside interests are – what they really aspire to? If you help them realise this – what will result for you and the business?

The ambitions of your staff don't have to be the same as your ambitions for the practice for them to be worth investing in. What is important for the business is that your staff are pulling in the same direction as you – and in the direction you want the firm to go. You therefore need to be aware of their aspirations, then you will be able to help them achieve them. Some may not have thought much about it themselves for some time, or they may not expect you to be asking, but if you know what they are aiming for, just imagine what a difference it would make to them if you helped them get there. You are in a position to help them in a number of ways, such as by giving encouragement or linking them to other people you know, but mostly by giving them some of your time. This will not only be to their advantage – creating a space in which a person can flourish will benefit the practice too, because as they gain something, they become a more valuable member of staff. People are happier if they feel valued and nurtured, enabling them to grow professionally.

In most situations, if people want to achieve something, they can ask someone for help. People are pretty much the same everywhere and most will not be able to resist offering advice or assistance in some way – they simply can't help themselves, and it makes them feel better too. However, as a leader in a work environment, don't expect staff to ask for your help. There may be a number of reasons why they won't, but most of them will be to do with confidence. Instead of waiting for a staff member to ask you for help, get them there faster by offering your assistance first.

Architecture already has a built-in understanding of the benefits of giving back to society, simply because we provide buildings in a public environment. Although we make each building specific to the client's brief, we recognise those buildings have a wider role to play in society. The arrangements for training architects similarly recognises the added value that a student benefits from during their year out, even if the value to the practice is unlikely to be felt (immediately at least) in terms of profit. It is widely understood by architecture practices everywhere that they have both a moral and a professional responsibility to train the next generation of architects, but there are broader benefits, reaching beyond the student and the practice, to them being trained well.

In other professions, especially in education, there seems to be an understanding of the value in encouraging staff to move around, so they will gain experience that will help them grow professionally. Perhaps this is easier in education because it is not a business, but this fluidity is rarely encouraged in architecture practices beyond student placements, and even here, practices will often try to keep their Part 2 students. I think a fluid approach to employment could be, and should be, introduced more widely because it will develop the skills of future architects and would encourage sharing of skills, particularly between small and larger practices.

Following the coronavirus pandemic and the normalisation of working from home, this may start to change. For example, an agile work policy could include provisions to make it possible for staff members to take a sabbatical. Sabbaticals are popular in other countries, particularly Australia, and offer much to broaden professional experience.

Measures to acknowledge emerging changes in attitudes to work should begin to be explored within the architecture profession in the UK. For instance, the RIBA Jobs job board might in future include an 'exchange' list, to help trainee or newly qualified architects consider a sabbatical in another practice for a single project or a specified period of time. A bit like the loan system in football, where larger clubs loan out promising new players to smaller clubs to teach them the lessons of the game across all levels, so larger practices could allow their promising recruits the opportunity to run a small project in another practice so they can learn new skills in a wider context. This could be a very powerful training experience, and the collaboration between practices could lead to other benefits.

Another, more quickly implementable idea is to provide an 'enrichment' offer to all staff. This might comprise offering to all staff up to a week per year of paid time off during which they would undertake an activity to 'enrich the soul'. The activity could be connected to work, but that's not really what this is about. Instead, staff can be encouraged to think more tangentially. It would be an opportunity for them to do something they haven't ever done because they've never found the time due to work. It doesn't need to be obligatory, and there should be no need for the person to make a presentation at the end. It is designed simply to offer space for professional growth. We recently started offering this opportunity in our practice and some of the activities so far have included an art class, golf lessons, a trip to a foreign art gallery, a field trip to study historic castles and a hedge-laying course.

Collaboration

When you are asked to take on a new project you may find you do not have a particular skill that will be needed or sufficient resources readily available. Collaborating with other practices can help you to overcome these deficits. It can also bring other benefits, such as providing an opportunity for you and your staff to work with different people, different projects and, usually, different sectors – or at least projects of different scale. This cross-pollination can potentially introduce new ideas, leading to increased energy and commitment due to the variety it can offer.

Collaboration will also bring demands, often onerous, but these can reframe opinions among staff on the way things should be done – or the way things have been done previously. This may provide you with an opportunity to review certain working methods, structures or systems that you have historically been following but which can be improved upon to everyone's benefit. It helps to keep staff engaged if, as well as enjoying the work they are doing, they have the opportunity to contribute to finding new ways to work. Retaining good staff is a key factor in maintaining steady growth because it provides the stable environment necessary for building momentum. As the practice's values start to become embedded in the way staff operate, the opportunity to develop ideas even further increases. These longer-term benefits feed into the sustainability of the firm, as well as the staff. Staff become more resilient if they can see that changes in their way of working improve their experience and increase the satisfaction they get from their work. The business benefits if it is not forced to recruit regularly just to bring in staff to fill gaps left by leavers.

Setting up a collaboration with another practice is not difficult. Stay in touch with as many practices as you can (RIBA networks are invaluable for this) and ask them critical questions, such as: How is your workload? Do you have enough staff? Are you planning to recruit? Have you ever thought about collaborating? You should also check what CAD packages other practices use, as it will be easier to collaborate if you use the same system.

Once you have agreed in principle to collaborate with another practice, you then need to agree the fee. This will normally be easier than you think – both of you know the value of your work and so settling on a figure can be a simple case of discussing it. You might offer to work on a reduced hourly rate or provide a lump sum for a package of drawings – just as you might vary fee proposals for clients according to the requirement of the work.

Depending on the nature of the project, you may supply your work with a 'white label', for the organising practice to badge with the drawing title they normally use when they issue their own drawings. Alternatively, you might agree to share the title, with both practices visible in the information exchanges. You should alert your PII broker to this new arrangement, but it need not increase your premium or expose you to any higher risk than you are already covered for.

Collaboration is obviously not limited by geography. Even before remote working became normalised during the 2020 coronavirus pandemic, technology allowed shared data environments to be employed by multiple users at the same time and for live draft drawings to be available for checking by others.

Once a collaboration is under way, the arrangement can be reciprocated. While it is unlikely that collaborations will continue without pause, over a period of time trust can grow between the practices involved. This leads to opportunities for sharing of training, software or information on new products, or even combining social activities, between the practices. This is especially beneficial for sole traders or smaller offices who practise near to each other, when this type of arrangement can lead to informal networks becoming established.
It may benefit each member of the group in a different way. For example, an architect may become more confident about being able to call on additional expertise should it be required, such as when a change in scope on a project demands resources or specialist knowledge that they are not able to provide. Collaboration should, of course, benefit all those involved. When there is a prospective new project which, if considered independently by one member, may be lost due to lack of resources or experience, being able to offer the combined skills and resources of several practices can win the project, keeping those practices in work. Which, at the end of the day, is what we all need to keep going.

Endnotes

1 Level 2 is equivalent to GCSEs at grades A* to C, Level 3 is equivalent to A levels, Level 4 is equivalent to BTEC professional diploma, and Level 5 is equivalent to higher national diploma (HND) or foundation degree level.

2 Kahneman, D. *Thinking, Fast and Slow* (London: Penguin, 2012).

3 Agarwal, P. *Sway: Unravelling Unconscious Bias* (London: Bloomsbury, 2021).

4 Forscher, P.S., Lai, C.K., Axt, J.R. et al. 'A meta-analysis of procedures to change implicit measures', *Journal of Personality and Social Psychology* 117(3) (2019), pp. 522–559.

5 Government Equalities Office. *The Equality Act, Making Equality Real* (Leeds: CDS, n.d.), pp. 18–19.

6 Home Office. *Inclusive by Instinct, Diversity and Inclusive Strategy 2018–2025* (London: Home Office, 2018), p. 4. Available at www.gov.uk/government/publications/diversity-and-inclusion-strategy-2018-to-2025 [accessed 23 December 2021].

7 Gill, S. *Successful Difficult Conversations in School* (Ipswich: John Catt Educational, 2018), pp. 103–109.

5

Clients

It can be easy to get things wrong with clients. But equally, it can be simple to get things right – you just need to keep in mind they are your business's primary source of money. If you pay close attention to the needs of your clients you will create the best chance for your business to remain profitable.

Getting paid is the difference between business survival and failure. Money may not be the reason you practise architecture, and it does not replace the broader value you can offer, but not receiving proper payment for your services is a perennial complaint among architects. We can do more to change this. For one thing, we should talk more about money and value. Recognising that we sell time has helped me to run an architecture practice. We should also accept that clients are our customers; identifying their requirements and tailoring the services we can offer to suit them does not mean we offer any less value or expertise. Rather, it means we provide people with what they want and what they need – and don't lose money doing so.

Help yourself by doing what your clients want – not what you want. Listen carefully to initial briefing instructions; you don't have to provide more than you were asked for to deliver good value. If you do what your clients expect of you, they are more likely to pay you for it.

A common cause of misunderstanding by clients is what is included in the price. If we don't differentiate when one action is over and the next one begins, we can't expect clients to define this for us. Help your clients understand what is included in the fee by invoicing regularly and at the end of each stage – this is the clearest signal you can send to a client about when a package of work has been finished. It can be surprising how rapidly clients will agree to sign off and approve a stage proposal if there is a bill accompanying it – especially if you make it crystal clear that any additional work to amend the proposal will be charged as an extra service.

The most important thing in managing client expectations is to be frank, honest and upfront about money at the beginning. Know the value of your work and don't be afraid to say what it is. This isn't always easy, and you may sometimes feel that it will impair your relationship. It won't. Remember, you are the expert your client has employed to help them realise their dream.

Private domestic clients come in all shapes and sizes, but they often know little about what you can actually do for them. It may be the first and only time they engage an architect. Architects are often the type of people who can't stop themselves from helping others – we probably give away for free as much as we charge for. Professional clients know this and try to take advantage of it (sometimes), but domestic clients come to expect it as a result of our behaviour. This is all wrong and will cost you a fortune. We are the only ones who can change it, and we must – but we don't, or we don't tend to.

At the end of the day, remember it's not your dream you're working on, it's your client's. Working with this understanding will help you to keep your business profitable, and resilience relies on you being paid.

Expectations

Not everyone thinks the same. What is satisfactory for one client won't get a second look from another. Aiming to produce work that is good enough to satisfy the client's expectations, rather than striving for the highest standards and the nth level of detail, can be a time saver and improve profitability. It does not mean you are delivering a lower quality service, it means you are providing the right service at good value.

Much will depend on the type of project, your client's level of experience and the sector they work in. Domestic clients have often never been involved in any development before and will be relying on you to 'teach' them the process. This will be demanding on your time, so it is worth identifying early on the difference between your architectural services and your liaison and reporting. Separating these activities in your fee schedule, to show how much time will be spent on each, makes it easier to highlight when you have reached the fee agreed. In turn, this should make it easier to ask for more money when necessary, or at least to put the brakes on the time you are spending. If you allow clients to think the work you are producing for them comes with a free tutorial on 'how to be an architect' and then you invoice them on a time-spent basis, the total cost will appear disproportionate to the amount of work you ended up producing for them, because it won't be more than you agreed, it just took longer, once you added in the oral manual describing what you did. You will also find that when you couple the provision of such detailed advice (to help the client understand the design and construction process) with the production of information required to achieve permissions, permits or prices, the fees you estimated for each stage will be woefully short.

In contrast, professional clients may not understand exactly what your services involve, but they will know what they want from you – which does not usually include an explanation of how things work in the construction industry. This leaves you time to deliver the service you originally priced. That's not to say working for professional clients has no watchpoints – it has many, but they are usually different from those to be aware of when working for domestic clients. For instance, professional clients will usually expect more from you than you have allowed for in your fee proposal. This is particularly true for revisions, which can be especially costly. To avoid spending even more unpaid time, in trying to justify the costs of the multiple changes, be sure to invoice promptly and peg these bills to your revision issues (see 'Time recording' in Chapter 2, page 26). Following the basic model of covering an information drop with an invoice removes at a stroke any doubt over what you have included in your fee agreement and what is extra.

On the reverse side, if a client thinks you have done more to explore an option or draw up a scheme they didn't say they wanted, you might be left carrying the cost of this work yourself. You or your staff may simply be doing what all architects are trained to do: explore the options, solve the problems and come up with solutions. However, not every client wants that – or they do, but they don't want to pay for it in their agreed fee and, if given the option, may not instruct you to do it if you offered it as an extra service. Clients want you to provide what they agreed to pay for.

Asking clients about different options, showing multiple feasibility studies, suggesting alternatives to their initial brief – when all you might be doing is attempting to add value – can light a touchpaper when you submit your invoice. Complaints such as 'I never asked you to look at so many options' or 'I told you exactly what I wanted at the outset' reflect how some clients assess the value of your service. They are not entirely wrong. When you take your car for an MOT, you don't expect to pay the garage for making improvements to the aerodynamics. Architecture is obviously not the same as vehicle maintenance, although the Egan Report made a strong case for the analogy,[1] but when clients or customers are paying for a service, they have a right to know they will be getting what they wanted. If you can add value without losing money doing so, then you have the makings of a successful business.

Being clear about the level of service you will provide – what it includes and what it doesn't – must happen at the outset. When providing a full service, we are by the side of the client and their project at the beginning, the middle and the end, which means it can be difficult for both parties to identify the completion of each stage of the work. A partial service will almost inevitably bleed from one stage into the next. For instance, a planning application will have several stages: at what point would you consider it complete? Upon submission, at validation, after supplying additional information to the local authority during the process or at determination? If your client has never submitted a planning application before, they will not know the different stages. These must be explicitly stated when the costs are being agreed, to avoid a client becoming disillusioned with your firm and so reluctant to pay you.

Issuing staged invoices throughout the planning application process is also critical for your cash flow. It is neither right for, nor of any benefit to, your accounts to wait until the determination of an application before you get paid for services undertaken several months earlier. Those fees represent assets due to you and the longer they take to reach you the more working capital you need – or, to put it bluntly, the longer you have to wait for the money, the more expensive it is and the more likely you are to go bust (see 'Working capital' in Chapter 1, page 9).

Be disciplined about the amount of time you spend on each activity and, at the start of each phase or RIBA Plan of Work stage, programme your time to stay within the agreed fee. Even if you don't anticipate charging separately for the activities, keeping track of them for your own records helps prevent you underestimating the amount of time all these aspects of a project will take. You can use the information the next time you start a similar project, to give you better information on its true costs.

The time required to prepare location plans, boundary drawings, design and access statements and block plans for a planning application can mount up. Physically assembling this information, along with additional information supplied by other consultants, such as bat surveys or contamination reports, to upload onto the Planning Portal will take longer than you want. This all represents time spent on the project that can and should be included in the fee.

By getting into the habit of recording activities stage by stage, the actual costs to the practice of each of the many stages of a project can more clearly be understood. This should also help you stay within the fee agreed by not exceeding the time and cost allocated to each project stage. If we allow ourselves to drift from one stage to another, we are working for nothing and so making the practice less profitable.

Agreement

Are you always certain you know precisely what your client wants? You can find you have wasted an awful lot of effort and money if it is only at the end, or when you bill them, that they tell you what they really wanted. It is critical that you set out for the client precisely your understanding of their brief and what they want you to do. Once you think you know what your client wants, ensure you include a description in your appointment letter to them – make this part of the document they sign. If they accept your offer to provide them with what they want, you have agreement. The agreement between you and your client is as much a record of their instructions to you as it is about how much you will charge. It is the common document everyone returns to when there is money to pay or a disagreement to resolve.

So how do you ensure you do understand what the client wants? You have to listen. Consider the following disastrous example from my early experience.

PRACTICE INSIGHTS

That's all we wanted...

I was a Part Two student working in Devon and had been given responsibility by the practice directors to meet some potential new clients. I arranged to see them in their small terraced cottage to take a look at the property and establish their brief. When I arrived, they asked me where I'd parked and we chatted about how it was a busy road and some people's cars had been damaged by passing traffic; one or two of their neighbours had even managed to turn their small front gardens into a driveway, but they didn't know how this had been possible because the council wouldn't let them do this when they'd asked. They told me they were thinking of an extension to provide a bigger kitchen – something with better access to the garden. They also thought, as they were extending out on the ground floor, they might as well have an additional first floor bedroom over the top. They definitely needed some more natural light as all the cottages had pokey windows and the kitchen faced north. They would like something modern, but not too modern – it had to be in keeping (the property was one in a modest, vernacular stone terrace of two-up/two-down cottages). I collected all this information and took a tour round, making some survey notes as I did so. Back in the office I checked my notes, prepared a summary of what they wanted and told the directors how long I estimated it would take me to do the job.

The commission was agreed and I set to work on the drawings for a two-storey extension with all the features they'd mentioned. Eager to please, I almost certainly overdid it on the options, and rather than preparing an initial feasibility study I had practically created a finished proposal before sending anything to the clients. So, having used up nearly all the fee, I sent them a draft option showing only a fraction of what I'd actually done and they said it looked great. Spurred on, I completed a full set of beautiful drawings (almost up to building regulations standard, even though we still hadn't submitted the planning application) and put these together with a planning application form and sent them off to the clients for any final comments. When there weren't any, I made the application to the council, successfully obtained a planning permission and this was sent with our invoice to the clients. It was then that they gave us notice they wouldn't pay, because they couldn't afford to build an extension and, anyway, we didn't get them permission to park off-road, on a new driveway in their front garden, which, they said, was 'all we wanted'.

When I look back over this, I see so many things that I do differently now it is almost impossible to know where to start listing my mistakes. But to focus on the key point about instructions, I could have done better at the outset if I had only listened. Learning to listen – to really listen – is the single most important part of running a business. Especially listening to clients when they are telling you what they want. Often, you will only learn what a client wants if you ask the right question – learning to listen is actually about being able to respond to what someone has said, and for that you have to have heard them. In this instance, the clients definitely talked about the parking, but, in my naïvety, I probably only heard what I thought they were saying. It's true they did talk about the other things as well, and they did agree to the drawings I sent them before making the planning submission, but at the end, when it all came out in the wash, they simply said they didn't understand the process. Why would they? They had never made a planning application before – that's why they came to us in the first place. They never built the extension.

Listening is a skill and it can be learned. You can easily test how well you listen by recording a conversation with someone (preferably not a client – stick to a colleague or a friend for this task) and then writing up your notes of what they said. Before you listen back, ask the colleague to compare your notes with their understanding of what they told you. Treat it like informal CPD. It can be illuminating for both parties – not only how well someone listens, but how clearly others explain themselves. Anyone who has been involved in a lot of initial briefing conversations will know you sometimes have to ask the same question multiple times and in different ways to find out what someone really wants – and before they will tell you.

You can help to prevent misunderstandings further down the line by clarifying the process for agreement at the initial briefing. Make it clear to clients what you will need them to agree to and when and, especially, that you won't start work or move onto the next stage until you have received agreement from them. It is not always obvious to clients what you want from them, when you want it, or even that you require them to approve each different stage. To obtain your client's approval might sometimes take twice the allotted time you estimated. Alternative ways of structuring fees – such as charging for providing drawings and then, separately, for meetings – usually helps clients make decisions more quickly, but issuing invoices almost always prompts a response.

When you establish your timescale for producing information, you should identify your preparation time separately from any periods of time the client will need for considering their agreement. This can be invaluable later, if someone is grumbling over the time it has taken to reach a particular point – usually a planning submission of some description. Being able to show that you produced your information on time means that any delay caused by the client can't reflect badly on you.

Reporting

Every client wants to be kept up to date, even if there is nothing to report. To achieve this, you first need to consider who is the best person to keep up the regular reporting – does it really have to be you, or even the project architect? Then, to make sure it happens, build this level of reporting into your office and project programmes (and your fee schedule too – liaison with the client can be time hungry and a fee drain).

Specialist customer relationship management (CRM) software is available for precisely this kind of project/client-related reminder service. CRM systems are mainly used by sales teams who make multiple calls each day to seek new leads for businesses and list out follow-up calls, sometimes months ahead, to hot prospects. If CRM software doesn't match the investment detailed in your strategic plan for your architecture practice,[2] applying the principle of coordinating specific project information and recording it chronologically in a central location is still worthwhile. This makes staying on top of lots of projects at different stages much more manageable. Being able to access information such as the date and time you called a client or they called you, or the expiry date of their planning permissions, without having to delve into each project file means you can list out different activities across multiple clients or projects (datasets). These activities might be reminders to submit a reserved matters application before the expiry of an outline planning permission, progress updates on project work or chasing for the client's approval of information issued. They will also help to avoid the issue of who is waiting for whom.

Architects could be accused of being slow to take up the 'customer relations' approach that has been a feature of most other businesses for years. This means there may be a side of your service that you're underinvesting in and which could help you to win work and secure financial stability for your practice. For instance, there is perhaps an expectation on our side as designers that when we send out drawings to clients they will respond with a schedule of comments and amendments. Many will do this as a matter of course, but not all clients realise they have a role to play in shaping the designs to suit their brief and they may need this to be explained to them in the early stages.

A key part of staying in touch during different stages of a project is to make the whole experience more enjoyable for your clients. This shouldn't just be applied to domestic clients; all clients want to enjoy the relationship they have with you, and many feel it gives them an opportunity to tap into their own creativity.

Anything you can do to help your 'customers' enjoy the process will boost your reputation and make it more likely you will get paid. It can be useful to think of your clients as customers, to whom you sell your time. This will help you to focus seriously on who in your practice is best suited to communicate with your clients – customer service skills are not within everyone's repertoire. It is common in a lot of practices for the project architect to be the default communicator with their client, but it doesn't have to be them. Identifying different skill sets within your staff can make it possible to use other members of your team to relay updates to clients in a way that benefits both your clients and your staff.

Think of regular progress reporting to clients as a self-preservation tactic too – a way of protecting your time. If you don't report regularly to the client, you risk being caught on the back foot. When a call comes in from someone you know is expecting to receive work from you and you haven't done it yet, you are vulnerable. This is exactly the moment when you might feel compelled to respond in a way that may cause problems for other committed project work or cause you to work more hours. This won't help you in the end, and it could destabilise your practice by affecting trust and reputation.

Fee bidding

At university, architecture is an art, and in practice, it becomes a craft, but your firm is a business – it sells your time to make money. Architecture is a service industry. You need to quantify projects in terms of the profit they will make you. It is not wrong to think this way – it doesn't tarnish your service. Think about the value of your service to each customer – what do they want and what will they pay for? You have to choose for them sometimes – not everyone knows what an architect does. You will understand the value you can add to every project, but don't expect your customers to understand this – they understand cost. It is up to you to tailor your delivery to what they want.

For any project, you will be required to submit a fee bid to the potential client, laying out the services you will provide and the prices you will charge for those services. There are already several books that can instruct you in how to prepare fee bids, so this section highlights only a few key things you need to think about.

There are few shortcuts to writing fee bids. This is where your time sheets, project records, sector analysis and historical invoice data come into their own. Time spent on the fee bidding process itself needs to be recorded – not so it can be charged to the client, but to ensure you allocate budgeted time in your own programme for this activity. This will also help you to see how much time you can save by carrying out previous project research, the intention being that the time you spend preparing fee bids will becomes less as you gather more data or find better ways to retrieve and interpret it. Using other members of staff in this process can be a real time-saver too. Once you have a system for recording time – one that allows interrogation of work stages, sector types and project budgets – staff whose time is normally included as an overhead can be trained in assembling the information needed to prepare each new bid.

Let's first break down what is involved:

1. An enquiry is made to your firm.
2. Your firm responds.
3. A consultation or meeting is held, which may or may not be on site.
4. You collect an initial brief.
5. You assess how much time you think it will take you to provide your services.
6. You assess when you could reasonably start.
7. You set out your fee proposal in a letter or a table of some kind.
8. You add the terms and conditions to be offered to this prospective client.
9. You and the client agree the terms.

Only once terms have been agreed can you start charging for the time you will spend delivering your service.

Table 5.1: Comparing time spent preparing fee bids in relation to project budget

Fee bid (hours)	Project budget (£000s)	Agreed fee up to Stage 3 (£000s)
38	850	25.48
6	400	6.75
0.5	20	1.45

Depending on the scale and complexity of the project you are bidding for, the list of nine activities above will usually take a minimum of two to three hours, but may run up to a number of days, or even weeks. Table 5.1 shows the amount of time our practice spent on the preparation of fee bids for recent projects of different sizes. This time was spent before the architect was appointed.

It was possible to spend only half an hour preparing one of the fee bids in Table 5.1 because other members of staff were involved who don't record all of their time – and it was for a very small project. Their involvement not only included preparing the initial documents, but also as many of the activities in the list above as possible. If you boil it down, you might only need to provide your unique expertise to activities 3 and 4. You should also think carefully about whether or not you need to make a site visit before you price the job.

If you link this thinking with the comments on customer services in the sections above then a different approach to fee bidding might start to emerge. This approach aims to capitalise on specific job roles within your team, using the complementary skills of individual members of staff to secure new work and deliver it. Anything you can do to reduce the amount of time spent in preparing bids will help your profitability, and using your staff to the best of their ability keeps them engaged.

The bid itself is your opportunity to set out not only the fee, but also the services you will be providing, as well as those you won't. The more information you can include at this point in the relationship between you and the client, the better it will be when it comes to you getting paid. The fee bid should be part of the document that will form your appointment with the client. The appointment is your contract. Depending on the nature of the project, you can use one of the various RIBA Professional Services Contracts or a letter of appointment. Think about how you can make the appointment document itself work harder for you if your bid is successful, by including a summary of the tasks and activities you propose to undertake at the different RIBA Plan of Work stages. Standard published contracts will include a list of services for you to amend and adapt. If you are appointed, this list becomes the list you should use in your time sheets, so you can record time spent against each of the activities agreed as part of the fee, which then links seamlessly into your invoicing. (See also 'Time recording' in Chapter 2, page 26.) If you use this method, the client will be able to see included on any invoice you send that the work done relates clearly and unambiguously to the fee agreement they signed.

Invoices will also need to differentiate between the agreed fee and subsequently agreed additional or extra services. As an example, under Stage 1 of the RIBA Plan of Work 2020, the description of activities includes 'Undertake Feasibility Studies'.[3] If you were to use simply this as a description in your fee bid, how many studies will your client expect? The answer is as many as are required, irrespective of how many comments and suggestions, revisions and amendments the client asks you to make. If you include sufficient time in your fee bid for this work – crack on. Alternatively, if you state in your fee bid the number of feasibility studies you have allowed for, 1, 2, 3 or more, you can claim extra fees for the amount over this number you end up preparing. Site visits and, especially, reporting back to the client (see 'Expectations' on page 76) should be treated in the same way. If you list out these items in your fee proposal, at the outset, you will make the rest of the project run more smoothly. If you experience push-back against your fee proposal, think how much easier it is to respond to it at the beginning of the project – before you have done any work – than when you are knee-deep in unclaimed charges for a spiralling workload. Protecting yourself against future claims may not seem a very positive way to start a new relationship, but it will benefit your business if you do by shielding you against unexpected financial shocks caused by non-payment of fees further down the line. Using standard forms of appointment will also offer protection by using tried and tested terminology, meaning it is less likely your contract leaves you exposed to an interpretation you did not intend.

Payment

What leverage do you have to ensure you get paid? There are appointment contracts, small claims courts and implicit terms, but if someone doesn't want to pay, even using these methods will not always guarantee you actually get the money.

First, make sure you invoice your clients for the work you have done. It seems so simple, but leaving an invoice until you get just one more thing done on the drawings is an easy trap to fall into. If you don't issue an invoice, you won't get any money. Prepare a straightforward invoice schedule, and share it with your client so they know when to expect to pay you. It need only list out the stages at which you will issue an invoice, but it can be extremely useful and helpful to refer back to when you come to send out invoices. There are also pro forma emails/letters you can use to follow-up the issue of an invoice and to remind

PRACTICE INSIGHTS

Unpaid fees

Some years ago we took a client to court over unpaid fees of around £10,000 and won the case. Then we received one five-pound note in an envelope from the client, after they had pleaded hardship to the court in a side case and a payment schedule of £5 per month had been agreed. It didn't seem to matter this would take over 150 years to settle. We never received another payment. To follow this up using the law would have resulted in even more solicitors' fees and wasted time, with no certainty of payment at the end. The whole episode leaves a bad taste in the mouth, but I was given a simple piece of business advice when I took over my firm: money comes in and money goes out. This truism has helped me on a number of occasions. In other words, 'stop counting and move on'.

the client about an approaching payment due date. These can be useful not only because they mean you don't need to spend time preparing a reason why an invoice needs to be paid (there is a temptation to over justify – see the 'Invoicing' box in Chapter 3, page 50), but also because they 'professionalise' your firm's accounting procedures.

The most reliable method for ensuring payment, however, is to send your invoice before you make any submission – especially a planning application. Use the submission as a lever: 'Once you've paid, we will make the application'. It is not always as easy to time this as people think, especially when your client is pressing hard for the submission to be made. And there's always a reason why you are made to feel up against it, such as changing legislation, an expiry date from a previous application, or even Christmas. If you can do it though, it is effective.

Having said it is not always easy to get paid, there are simple steps you can take to improve your chances, such as always printing 'Preliminary' or 'Draft' on any drawings issued up until the point you have been paid for them. Stating clear timescales at the outset of the project will protect you against the possibility of being held to account over a delay you did not cause (see above). Think about pushing back on client deadlines – find out who set them and how fixed they really are. It is not uncommon to receive a demand from someone in an unseemly rush to get something prepared to meet a looming deadline, when after only a few questions it becomes obvious that the pressure can be almost immediately relieved by making one phone call to whomsoever to confirm that something is going to be done, but that it will take some time and so can there please be an extension? To which the answer is yes.

Second, relate any invoice to the work the client agreed to pay you for. If you can closely match the invoice description to the appointment agreement (see 'Fee bidding' on page 82), it will be harder for a client to dispute the amount. The description can be what you choose depending on the service you are offering, but it should be straightforward and unambiguous, such as 'x' hours of consultancy, a site visit, a particular issue of drawings, an application to the local authority, etc. However, avoid including too much information in a description, as this can give your client an opportunity to quibble over the precise wording to challenge the amount.

Where you have concerns about 'scope creep', make sure you alert your client to the extra costs applicable before you do the additional work. Everyone else in the office has to be mindful of this too – it is likely to be your biggest loss of fees. Paying close attention to time sheets, job diaries, work schedules and stage budgets is crucial for picking this up, but make sure you have a clear process for bringing this to your client's attention quickly. It can be difficult to extract the cost of additional work from all the other information that has built up in the middle of the job, but it is fundamental and will be reflected in your turnover. Just as contractors have clear procedures for pricing extras, so must we. Consider how much effort we spend on variations and architect's instructions when we administer a building contract – it's all about pricing extras. So, do the same with your own work.

Third, stay in touch with your client. Keep communication lines open at all times, even when it might be awkward. It can help to have more than one point of contact with the client, such as one person for providing the architecture service and another for talking about the money. It is obvious, but effective. A possible arrangement would be for two colleagues within the practice to share the communication on each other's projects, but for this to work they would obviously need an understanding of the issues relating to both projects (see also 'Transparency' in Chapter 4, page 60). It can also pay to be more reasonable than you really want to be. You have more chance of getting paid if you can keep talking. Sometimes it is worth easing off the pressure and offering alternative payment terms, such as phased or scheduled instalments. Perhaps you can identify one particular area the client is unhappy about, in which case, offer to set part of the payment due to one side just until you can interrogate the specific amount, but in the meantime the client should settle the remainder. You need the money in your account, so it's better to get some of it in (preferably the bulk of it) and then consider the effort required to secure the rest.

You can review the payment terms at any point, provided both parties agree. For instance, if a project is on site and ad hoc visits or design information are required, but you have endured a history of late payments from the client throughout the project, you might consider offering alternative terms that would benefit both sides. These could be: up-front bullet payments for each issue raised; irregular but rapid invoicing to suit the time involved, e.g. at the end of the week in which you were called to site; running 'taxi meter' style invoicing, with an invoice issued at the end of each month; or billing queries by number and the time spent on each. If these methods are employed, the client will be able to see the cost of every involvement and you are more likely to be paid promptly, preventing a build-up of fees arising from many different and separate incidents.

Fourth, be patient. Building a business is about building a reputation. Having a good reputation is one of the most reliable ways to bring new business through the door. As a form of marketing, you could think of it as your 'background ventilation' – always there, always keeping you healthy; whereas a targeted advertising campaign is 'purge ventilation' – direct action to deliver a fresh intake. It is important to be firm about being paid, but demonstrating reasonableness will go a long way. Remember also where the money comes from. Just as clients have different expectations according to their experience or the sector they are operating in, different types of client draw on different sources of money. A commercial client may be allocating percentages from an investment fund; a developer is more likely to be committing tranches borrowed across a time period; whereas a domestic client might have the whole project budget in the bank after saving up for years. The amounts involved will vary considerably between each of these examples, likely being much smaller for the domestic client, but the value to each client group is the direct reverse of the quantum. While none of them will want to spend more than they have to (especially not on your fees), the money from a private domestic client is most likely to be theirs – real money. Domestic clients are also the least likely to be able to accommodate an increase in budget. Take this into account when setting fees in the first instance. Domestic clients will rarely be able to find more money easily during a project. Being realistic about budgets at the outset will also help to ensure you get paid.

Finally, remember that sometimes a deal is the best solution. You need to consider the competing demands on your time. Pursuing payments is not quick, especially if you have to pick over time sheets and job diaries to justify hours spent. Take a close look at the amounts in question, cost your time for resolving the matter – and remember, the time you spend on a payment issue is time you spend *not* doing something else – think truthfully about whether or not you could have been quicker in delivering the work, and compare the actual cost to break even alongside the billing rates. Don't be afraid to make an offer – it can be useful to start with a 50:50 split and negotiate from there. It is painful, but swift. It also means you are more likely to be able to work with that client on future projects. And while you might think you never want to work with them ever again, remember how relationships are built – through shared experiences, through both good and less good times. Ultimately, your business is dependent on your relationships with people.

Endnotes

1 Sir John Egan chaired a taskforce for the government on the UK construction industry, resulting in the publication of *Rethinking Construction* in November 1998. Sir John was previously CEO of Jaguar Cars and parallels were drawn between car manufacturing and the production of buildings. Following on from the publication of the Latham Report (*Constructing the Team*) in 1994, *Rethinking Construction* was instrumental in catalysing change in construction, helping to bring BIM into government contracts.

2 CRM software does have a larger role to play in practice and can be used to implement sophisticated marketing campaigns and to manage specific customer requirements (to ensure when any member of your team contacts a client, they are aware of important matters), and, more generally, it will act as an intelligent database. Primarily, though, it was developed for dealing with the management of leads and new customers, and while it is always possible your practice has a flood of new enquiries, unless this is sustained for a prolonged period of time, investment in a CRM system may be difficult to justify. You should always relate any investment expenditure back to your strategic plan, however; if CRM fits in with your development goals, don't let me stand in your way.

3 RIBA. *RIBA Plan of Work 2020* (London: RIBA, 2020). Available at: www.architecture.com/-/media/GatherContent/Test-resources-page/Additional-Documents/2020RIBAPlanofWorktemplatepdf.pdf [accessed 18 January 2021].

6

Consultants

As an architect, you will rely on many different consultant outfits to provide you with support on your projects, such as in the preparation of planning submissions, building regulations applications and tender packages. Developing relationships with these various organisations and the individuals within them is critical if you are to build up a network of co-professionals. The benefits of these informal 'collectives' are manifold. Not only can they become a source of new work (through recommendations), but they also become part of your delivery team, and will help you to develop the credibility necessary for growing a reputation. In the same way as clients frequently want your recommendation on the best builder to use, they also rely on you to steer them towards the best and most appropriate consultants for the successful completion of their projects.

As you build a network of reliable and varied experts around you, your clients' trust in your firm's ability to deliver a quality service also grows. To do this involves getting to know the skills and strengths of these consultants and understanding how they do their work. They are the architect's equivalent of a contractor's supply chain. It is worth remembering that you will probably use them again and again over the course of your career, even if there are sometimes long gaps in between. This professional relationship is not the same as your relationship with your clients, both those who only require your services once and those who you will work with over several projects.

Your bond with other consultants is a close one because you both work for money from the same project purse. Consultants rely on multiple projects to sustain them, just as you do, which means they are bound to fair delivery of their services across all of the projects they are involved with, without favouring one over another. This binds you not only to the common purpose, but also to each other. When a project comes under stress, this relationship can be vital for finding a way forward. There will be times when you need to lean on each other to deliver tough messages during a project, such as having to provide unpopular advice to clients. Or sometimes, when you just need a sense check on a decision you have made or need to make, asking for the opinion of a co-professional who understands the project, the client and the contractor can bring real benefit.

Delivery

One of the main questions architects are asked in domestic work (and sometimes by commercial clients) is whether we can 'recommend a good builder'.[1] Similarly, you will be relied upon to know the right people to provide the right advice at the right time, although, in this instance, your client may not even be aware they need the expert views of another consultant. When working on domestic projects, it is rare to find a client who knows which arboriculturist they wish to use, or even what one is – let alone what they do and why one is needed for their project.

Being able to select an appropriately qualified consultant on behalf of your client matters because the client is relying on you to deliver their project. Finding the right people is part of your service. The consequences of this are that the performance of anyone you suggest becomes your concern. If, for instance, the arboriculturist's report is late, it can hold up the submission of your planning application and consequently the payment of your fee. This will reflect poorly on you if you were the one who suggested to your client to use them in the first place.

The onus is on you to make sure you do everything in your power to ensure the consultants you are relying on have everything they need, along with all the project information you can supply, to allow them to do a good job in a timely manner. Think of it like a contractor's supply chain – it is invariably the case that contractors do not provide their subcontractors with all the project information available. In almost every situation when a subcontractor is underperforming on site, if you talk directly to them they will tell you: (a) they do not have any drawings; (b) they don't have all the drawings; or (c) they only have A4 copies of excerpts of some A1 drawings, which don't show a key, a scale bar, a specification or annotations, or any of these things. If they don't have the full picture, it's no wonder they are underperforming. When you suggest a consultant to your client, it is in your interest to make sure you don't do what contractors do with their subcontractors.

When briefing the design team, you may need to spend a little longer briefing external consultants than you would with the in-house team members. You need to be certain you have given them the opportunity to ask the right questions before they prepare their submission. Ensure you provide them with a complete package of project information, otherwise there is the possibility of them sending a request to you for further information just moments before you were expecting the final report.

It is common for architects to appoint consultants on behalf of clients, and this can mean – certainly on smaller projects – there is little or no communication between them and the client. A consultant's relationship with the project and their understanding of what is required are established because of you and through you. Their input, although valuable, may also only be fleeting – a few days' work and then their involvement could be over. This time frame does not provide them with the luxury of being able to grow with the project, gather information and refine their input into it. Instead, your consultant may have only one part to play, and then the project is over for them.

While you may feel you are putting in a disproportionate effort to make the consultant's input the best it can be, it is worth it. For instance, if the report you commissioned doesn't include the most up-to-date design changes, you may end up spending more time searching for a remedy later; or if a protected species emergence survey didn't include the outbuildings, you may get an unwelcome shock after the hibernation season has started and you have to tell your client they will have to wait another six months for an updated report. Making this extra effort will mean you deliver a better overall service to your client. All taken together, this means you are more likely to get paid and you improve your chances of working on other projects for the same client, or even on projects with other clients as a result of their recommendation. It is also more likely the consultant will have enjoyed working on the project as well – because they had all the information they needed to work from – which makes them more likely to think of you should their work bring them into contact with another project requiring an architect.

Flexibility

When appointing consultants, you should try to find out how they operate in their work setting, as this may be different from how you work. Many will tackle their workload in series (one project after another). This method of working means that, when carrying out the work for your client on your project, they must have everything they will need in front of them before they start, and they will then not do anything else until it's finished. It also means that when they issue their draft to you, you need to read and review it straight away. If you need revisions to be made but don't inform the consultant immediately, you may find they have started another project and are not able to get back onto yours for a while. It can be a bit like trying to get another window delivered to site after the supplier delivered one of 24 units incorrectly assembled – never mind that it was their mistake, you just have to go back into their uncompromising 12-week fabrication queue and wait for your order to go through the factory again.

Most architects can only dream of being able to carry out their projects in series. Being able to work on just one project to completion, send it off to someone else and then issue your invoice just doesn't really ever happen in an architecture practice. Architects' projects tend to run in a complex system matrix, and it always seems that the amount of work to be done equals the square of the number of projects running in parallel!

These contrasting approaches mean it is not uncommon to find that the work of other construction professionals is programmed differently to the way architects programme their own work. As noted under 'Resourcing' (in Chapter 2), an architect's resource planning necessarily requires, as a repeating feature, a built-in hiatus to accommodate such activities as client consideration time, planning permission processes and tender periods. Where other consultants are able to prepare their work up to issue and then freeze their services, an architect's services are not so much frozen as kept in the fridge to be snacked on in the middle of the night. In fact, it can feel as if we are permanently on call to respond to everything everyone else needs.

There is an important distinction to make here between feeling like you are doing everyone else's bidding and being recognised as the lead consultant on a project. Getting paid to provide these services is the principal difference – if you set your appointment terms up correctly, to ensure your time is properly reimbursed, being lead consultant will be rewarding, in both senses of the word. Understanding the way other consultants work and provide their services will result in you delivering your services better and more efficiently, reducing the likelihood of you being drawn into costly corrections and time-consuming renegotiations.

As well as understanding the way other consultants plan their work, do you really know what they actually do and how they do it? In a detailed way? It can be a great help to properly appreciate the various factors other professionals need to consider before they can commit to an opinion. It is quite common for an architect to have a reasonably clear idea of the work of a topographical surveyor or a structural engineer – even if their calculations can be difficult to follow. Just like any subject, though, the more you know about it, the more there is to find out. This is not a call for you to become qualified in everything, it is simply saying that you should look for ways to become more acquainted with the activities and expertise of your colleagues and co-professionals. You can then use this understanding to help you shape your brief to them for each project.

It is worthwhile arranging informal CPD sessions with those from different disciplines, to talk about precisely these things. Most people are quite willing to talk about what they do, and even enjoy it. It is likely they will want you to reciprocate in some way, which can become a valuable way to network. Yuli Cadney, formerly of Rogers Stirk Harbour + Partners, then BDP and now a director at Kay Elliot, once said she always advised her students to 'build their alliances early'. This is such good advice. Your professional relationships with other consultants will be very rewarding – and can sometimes provide you with lifelines.

Reliability

To protect yourself from complaints from clients who are unhappy with information ultimately provided by an external consultant, you need to be rigorous during the consultancy tender process. If the consultant's work does not meet the client's demands, it will become your problem because you were tasked with briefing them. Clients will see you as the person who introduced these professionals into the design team, meaning you become responsible for what they produce – even when you have appointed them on behalf of your client and it is the client who is paying them for their services. It is difficult to charge for the time you might have to spend to rectify a situation like this, but you can charge for the time required to prepare the service brief at the time of the consultant's appointment.

If you appoint a consultant directly to provide their services on one of your projects, they become a subconsultant to your practice. I have always felt it is better to encourage your client to appoint a consultant directly, even if you arrange the appointment for them by preparing the brief and obtaining competitive quotes. The benefits of doing this are that it simplifies your VAT payments (if you are registered for VAT) and the client is owed a duty of care from the consultant directly – not through your practice – so if there is underperformance or negligence by them, the client can deal with them directly. Critically, the consultant will be covered by their own PII – not yours. It is good practice to keep a register of insurance cover held by other consultants who you approach to work with on projects, to ensure you know what protection your clients will be afforded – you will do this for contractors before they sign a building contract, so it should be no different with your co-professionals. You should ideally set a minimum level of cover, commensurate with the size of projects you tend to work on, and keep the register updated each year.

A briefing at the appointment stage, which might be at Stage 1, presents a perfect opportunity to assemble a pre-construction information pack, as part of your responsibilities under the CDM Regulations. Issuing the design team with a folder brimful with surveys, asset plans, briefing information, objectives and anything else to illustrate the scope and reach of the project means you will also have given them the best chance to perform well. It doesn't matter if you provide more than they might need to carry out their service, because for them to have the whole picture means they can choose to review the information specific to them and they will have access to background information should they need it. It also means you can more easily have a conversation with them about the other work that might be taking place – design team meetings are easier when everyone is able to see the complete picture.

The fact that you, as the architect, will probably be engaged on the project for longer than any other consultant puts you front and centre in the client's sights if things go wrong. If another consultant's information is incorrect, the client will expect you to have checked it, or if a consultant can't get their report completed in time, the client might think you haven't supplied them with the information they needed in a timely fashion. If it was worse, and the client felt the specialist consultant wasn't capable of doing the work, you may be tarnished by association because your professional relationships form part of your service offer, and the performance of the design team reflects on you.

These situations do occur, things do go wrong, and you can become embroiled in unsavoury matters, such as non-payment of the fees of others. In such moments, being able to turn to your records of the information you supplied, your briefing meeting notes and a timeline of how long it took you to respond to questions raised can be invaluable, so make sure you take notes and keep them.

Having long-standing working relationships with other construction professionals – based on understanding how they work, what they do and what they need to do it – might not prevent these situations from arising, but, when they do, your response is made easier and will be more effective. Incidents like this can happen at any point during a project and on a project of any size. Your reaction time is crucial. The issue will do doubt occur just at the moment you don't want it to, but it is at that precise moment you must act in order to survive. Being transparent with the design team, the contractor and the client about the particular issue – without attributing any blame – is made simpler when an atmosphere of trust, openness and respect for one another has been present from the beginning. To understand completely the issue that has arisen will usually require the expertise of all members of the team. You need them to be available and willing to contribute quickly, so that together you can form a rapid assessment and prepare a plan of action. Taking time to invest in those around you is always worth it.

Suitability

Just as you may not be tooled up for every type of architectural project on offer, other consultants will have strengths in certain areas and not others. If you don't know what a particular consultant likes or wants to work on, try asking them. The main reasons for preferring particular types of work tend to do with scale, location and time, but equally there may be other reasons why certain projects don't work for some consultants, such as use of BIM or other layers of emerging technology (e.g. point cloud laser scanners, drone pictures etc.). In the same way that you wouldn't put Tier 1 contractors in a tender against Tier 3 contractors, the same approach can be applied when requesting quotes from consultants. Quotes take time for everyone to prepare, and they are a service not usually paid for. Giving fair competition to all firms in any pricing competition is good practice, so you should understand who to approach according to the type of project.

Consultants' responses can be telling, but they often include only the price and when the work can be done. But is that because it was all you asked for? Price should be seen as just one element to present to the client. Obviously price is critical, but you might consider asking for fee bid returns to include answers to project-specific questions. These could be focused on sustainability, such as asking structural engineers for measurements of overall steel weights to be calculated and included in the project proposals, or on improved clarity, such as asking ecologists whether they would attend a client meeting to present their findings. The additional requirements that you include in the tender process should either offer value to the project or reduce the amount of time you will have to spend explaining to the client (particularly a domestic client) the implications of a consultant's findings. Explaining the process of design to a new client can be very time-consuming and quite unproductive, but it is even more onerous to have to do this for someone else's field of expertise. Including your consultants in this process adds value by bringing their specific expertise to the forefront and helping to create a sense of ownership of the project. Improving the relationship between you – including the other members of the design team and other people you work with – and the client makes good business sense. It is more likely to bring the best out of those involved and make the project more enjoyable for everyone.

Ambition

Chapter 1 talked about the importance of the *vision* and the *mission* for your business, where your direction of travel is laid out for everyone to see, along with what your purpose is and what you want to achieve in the future. There is no better opportunity to share this vision than when you are building relationships with other consultants. Do you know what their vision or mission is? They may not have one, but if that is the case, they are more likely to think about what it might be if you share yours with them and ask them about what they want their business to achieve. Do their goals align with yours? There may be a mutual benefit to working on a series of projects together if they do. It could even help to refine your own business planning if, through those projects, you see new opportunities to develop your understanding about how you can achieve your objectives.

It can often feel as if there is no time to talk about matters such as these, but it is usually simply a case of deciding to go first. The easiest way to start is by telling someone about what you have been doing or planning in relation to writing a vision, or how you have been reviewing your website. You can then ask them to say what they have thought about or discussed within their firm. Have they started yet? If they haven't, do they know what they would include? Or have they got a plan to prepare something? Having conversations like this in between specific project work can really benefit a working relationship. Don't be afraid to ask searching questions. You can find out a lot about the people themselves, and maybe even to mutual benefit.

You have something of an advantage here; you already have skills for eliciting a brief out of your clients and you can use the same set of skills to build a solid working relationship with those around you. Sometimes you can learn something new about a person even after you have been working with them for some time. People are endlessly fascinating, and you are a very lucky person if you are an architect. In your role you have the privilege of being able to work with every type of person, from domestic and commercial clients to civil servants in local authority, builders in small and large firms, subcontractors and other consultants, even sometimes other architects, and every one of them has some kind of ambition. Now, work out your ambition, write it down, agree it with your staff and go out there, make money and enjoy every aspect of running a successful, resilient business.

Endnote

1 You will often be warned not to 'recommend' the services of specific firms to your clients. This is because if you do, and the service provided is of poor quality, you may become liable in some way. As the qualified expert, your recommendation matters. Remember also that you have working relationships with several consultants, builders and professionals – do you really want to say that one is better than another? Or is it more likely that some are more suited to specific projects than others?

Appendix A

Case studies

Eight practices were approached to participate in the case study in Chapter 2: 'Time sheets and resource planning'. They were selected to reflect a broad cross-section of size and location across England. Six practices responded to say they would be willing to take part. A questionnaire was sent to each of them, and a follow-up telephone call made to run through the process. All respondents said they were happy for their answers to be published in full here and I am grateful to them. The analysis included in Chapter 2 is my interpretation in relation to the specific topic in the chapter. This unfiltered list of answers will hopefully provide more detail that may be of specific interest to some readers.

	Vagdia and Holmes Chartered Architects	**Gbolade Design Studio**	**The Bazeley Partnership Chartered Architects**
Respondent's name and position	Dhiran Vagdia, Director	Tara Gbolade, Co-Founding Director and Lanre Gbolade, Co-Founding Director	Martin Back, Consultant
Number of people employed	5	6	12
Location: city	Coventry	London	Bude
Practice structure (e.g. Ltd, LLP, partnership)	Limited company	Private limited company	Limited company
Date incorporated (if relevant)	1 October 2007		2012
Method used for time recording/ time sheets (if any) (e.g. name of software)	Manually entered spreadsheets.	TimeSheet plugin integrated with staff Google Calendars.	Web-based app called Harvest – a time-tracking management tool, including invoicing, expenses, projection, scheduling and programming. The programme is very versatile and can be set up and edited as required.
Increments of time recorded (e.g. 15 minutes, 1 hour etc.)	30 minutes (minimum)	15 minutes	Any amount of time can be configured against any project/work tasks. The minimum time set for TBP is 18 minutes, with increments of 30, 45, 60 minutes.
Do you record time spent on non-fee-earning work? (e.g. 'house accounts', prospects, staff meetings etc.)	Yes – for tentative projects and office administration.	Yes, by deduction of time spent on fee-earning project work against contracted working hours per week, and time-sheet recording of non-project work/tasks/activities.	Yes, we do, so that we have a complete picture and record of all non-project work done. Everything has a cost/time, and we can evaluate/measure all costs and time spent and determine at the end of each financial year what our base running costs are and whether or not we need to increase [or decrease] our overheads element within our fee structure.
What information is recorded with time records (if any)? (e.g. RIBA Plan of Work stage, activity etc.)	All time matters are recorded against a RIBA code and/or a unique office-based code, say for tentative projects.	Activities, tasks and RIBA stage. Staff (associates) responsible for the project and activities/tasks. Total project hours spent in a week per project. Total fee-earning hours spent per staff member. Total non-fee-earning hours spent per staff member per week.	As a project is commissioned, the project title [client name and brief description] TBP job number and the RIBA stages applicable are entered under the project. The entry is then assigned to those who will be working on the project. A time sheet can be opened by a staff/team member and time recorded against the project is entered every day. Within the project entered, and once the RIBA stage is entered, a drop-down dialogue box offers a range of tasks relevant to the RIBA stage presented. So, for example, at Stage 2 a client meeting or internal meeting can be recorded, or a site visit or communications recorded, etc. Another entry is also available for administration, non-project time, leave and speculative time [time spent on enquiries].

Willmore Iles Architects Ltd	Buttress Architects	rg+p
Paula Willmore , Founder Director	Gavin Sorby, MD	Robert Woolston, Director
28	65	85
Bristol	Manchester	London, Birmingham, Leicester
Limited company	Limited company	Initially a partnership established in 1979, and then incorporated as a limited company in 1999.
30 September 1999	2006	1979
Deltek	CMap	A computer record management system (CRMS) called CMap. CMap acts as a project management system, allowing us to record time and resource across job stages and also plan cash flow and invoicing points.
15 minutes	15 minutes	15 minutes
Yes.	Yes, everybody records this, apart from accounts and general admin staff. We have project codes and internal codes for admin. Potential projects have a project code as any other. We can filter by project stage or by zero confirmed fee. We monitor the amount of potential project work each quarter in terms of number and cost.	Yes, for example: research, quality system, networking, CPD, community/charitable work; bids and initial at risk work are also included.
The time sheets record project time under RIBA stages. Within each project this can also be allocated against: project time, bid time, BIM, meetings, site visit, speculative, travel. Reports for these activities can be extracted from Deltek on a project-by-project basis or company wide. Time sheets also record non-job time within the following categories: accounts, general admin, 1:1s, client development, CPD, EOT, H&S, HR, ISO, IT, marketing, non-chargeable, internal office meetings, recruitment, WIA2.0 (leadership project – succession planning). Reports for these activities can be extracted from Deltek on an individual or group basis.	Project stage or activity, depending on how the project has been set up and which template has been used.	Stage activity. Recorded against job stages as previously inputted into CMap, which usually follow the RIBA stages unless the project demands a different approach.

Table continues

	Vagdia and Holmes Chartered Architects	Gbolade Design Studio	The Bazeley Partnership Chartered Architects
What do you use the records for? (e.g. invoicing, future pricing, project monitoring etc.)	We use the records for recording time spent on jobs, and for reflecting on for future fee proposals. All members of the team are encouraged to access time sheets regularly, to learn and to continuously improve themselves.	Invoicing purposes; managing project progress against master Project Pipeline; as a gauge for future bids and fee proposals.	Harvest allows us to enter the fee amount for each RIBA stage. As time spent against each stage is entered, it easily allows those working on the project to manage time against fee efficiency. This can be done in a number of ways, but we all tend to bring up a simple bar chart graphic that plots time spent against the total fee time and a percentage anywhere along the time line. What it also does is issue an alert when 80% of the fee time has been spent. Staff can then manage the remaining fee time against remaining tasks in order to prioritise the remaining tasks or seek assistance/additional resource where a deadline is critical. At weekly programming meetings all staff are asked to flag up pressure points and 80% notifications so that a reassessment can be made of remaining tasks to ensure best efficiency outcomes.
Do you collate project records from each member of your staff? If so, how?	These are manually collated when appropriate, but, to be fair, usually our office members work exclusively on projects.	Yes, the main tool for capturing project records and progress is the weekly team huddle on Monday mornings, as well as recording staff project progress in the pipeline reporting schedule. We also have client design change trackers that we use to control and monitor design creep for invoicing purposes.	Yes, as described above. Each staff member is responsible for recording their time spent and actions/tasks against each project stage. If this falls behind, a notification is generated by Harvest to prompt the staff member. At the end of a project, Harvest can produce a simple or more comprehensive summary/overview of the project progress. This is invaluable in assessing whether methods of working need to change, especially against the backdrop of changes in IT, working practices, new emerging tasks and so on. While we don't want to become obsessed with time/task recording, 'what gets done, gets measured' and so can inform and steer a practice.
What method (if any) do you use for preparing your office programme? (e.g. name of software)	We use Excel to plan cash flow, forecasts and job progress, and to record forward projects.	A multi-linked and tabbed Excel spreadsheet, which reduces human error and the need for duplication of information. For sharing project progress with clients, we use an online programming platform specifically for architects and construction professionals called briq. works to deliver high-level RIBA stage progress updates.	We have tried Microsoft Office 365 OneDrive, but have in the end developed our own version to include all the features and methods of assessment we want out of a programming system that supports our ways of working. Lists of staff members and their assigned projects over days/weeks and other usual data are reviewed at a weekly programming meeting and adjustments made to resourcing as necessary. We use Harvest to inform this assessment and then monitor the updates made throughout the working week.

Willmore Iles Architects Ltd	Buttress Architects	rg+p
We use these records for: project monitoring, profitability monitoring, productivity and review for future fee bidding.	Invoicing, project monitoring, KPIs, utilisation, profit and loss. We have a comprehensive range of KPI charts that are all driven from CMap time sheet reports.	Invoicing, project and milestone monitoring, resourcing and project profitability.
Each project is entered into Deltek with a unique project number. All client resource and fee information is entered into the software and it is broken down into RIBA Stages 1–7. We also have a project quality plan which sits under our ISO 9001 and 14001 requirements, and this is updated regularly by the project architect. This is led by an associate under the senior leadership team (SLT).	It is available through CMap as a standard report if required.	This is done automatically, and reports are generated by the CRMS.
Deltek provides us with all the project information.	CMap	A combination of CRMS (CMap) for project-specific milestones and stages. On a more general office basis, we use a simple bespoke Excel worksheet split between the different architectural teams, which not only works as a shorthand project programme but also enables the entire company resource availability or clashes to be monitored.

Table continues

	Vagdia and Holmes Chartered Architects	Gbolade Design Studio	The Bazeley Partnership Chartered Architects
What do you call it? (e.g. office programme, resource plan etc.) Who sees it? (e.g. directors, management, team leaders, everyone)	'Deliverables Forecast', and all can see this information. The director is specifically allowed to view the cash flow forecast.	Our intelligent Excel spreadsheet is called the 'Project Pipeline'. It is visible to all project staff, but controlled and managed by the Studio Manager.	Just 'office programme', which is printed out each week and reviewed in the weekly office meeting where all staff and directors meet to review and discuss a range of matters. We also use this time to come together as an office, not least to hear from one another what each person is working on, what particular issues they have and if any help is required. It's also a good opportunity to exchange ideas and for all to make any kind of suggestions about how we work or how we might change something for the better.
Does your programme relate to your time sheets/records? If so, how?	It does relate to time sheet records, but only by manual cross-referencing. This is done on purpose at this time, to encourage everybody to understand the data and its implications.	The Project Pipeline is complemented by the time sheets, but they are not currently linked.	Yes, the RIBA stage time is projected in the programme against each project stage. It is not directly linked to the Harvest app. We prefer to discuss and assess each programme/progress with all staff and understand why certain things might or might not be happening, rather than viewing a simple electronic record that does not necessarily tell you the background to an issue.
In what increments of time do you programme tasks or activities for yourself/other staff?	30-minutes tasks.		Same for all as noted above. Obviously charge out rates per hour vary across staff and directors.
Do you assess actual time spent against programmed time?	Yes, continually, and this forms part of a cyclical review of tasks and time taken for tasks at any particular time.	Not nearly as often as we should do, but this is something we are working on implementing.	Yes, Harvest does this automatically and presents a snapshot or overview at any time as to where we might be in project efficiency. Then lessons can be learned, and adjustments made to ways of working and future fee proposal assessments.
Do you refer to your programme, project records or historic time sheets to help you prepare fee bids?	Yes, we do continually.	Yes, especially for larger projects, as the project programme and scope can often creep beyond what was originally proposed, so these reviews help provide a reality check against the client's brief and programme estimations.	Yes, particularly for larger projects or those that are complex. It provides us with a layer of understanding across the board, as well as the usual layers of fee calculation, so that hopefully we value our service and experience as accurately as we can and, if commissioned, have a good chance of delivering the quality of outcomes and making a profit!

Willmore Iles Architects Ltd	Buttress Architects	rg+p
We have few key monitoring spreadsheets: financial data in our 'financial toolkit', which SLT reviews monthly and all inputs to Deltek are used; work in progress (WIP) spreadsheets – input by project architects and checked with directors; BD projections forecast, for all projects – assessed against likelihood; SLT review; Project Pipeline worksheet – for discussions. Monthly office meetings give project updates and some very high-level business feedback. Quarterly EOT meeting for all staff includes a company update.	'Resource Plan', and all project managers can see it and resource their projects.	'Resource Plan'. Directors, team leaders and project managers can all review the CMap and resource plan. The plan is reviewed at a weekly resource meeting. Ultimate responsibility for resolving resource issues falls between one of our associate directors and a director responsible for resource.
Yes, indirectly – see above.	Not in a forward-looking way, but we monitor actual against planned on a project-by-project basis. Our project managers have access to this.	The Resource Plan shorthand programme should always reflect the details of individual project programmes and milestones that are established in CMap, which are monitored and reviewed regularly.
It depends on the nature of the project. A large scheme may have a member of staff full-time for 3–6 months. This will be in the Deltek resource programme. Other projects are resource-based and can be priced on an hourly rate. This will then be resourced accordingly.	We can choose hours or days based on the size of task appropriate to that project. Some of our projects are very small and some are very large.	We programme in half-day increments on the resource programme.
We are now in the process of looking at WIP for all projects. This will allow us to look at monthly activity against invoiced. We hope to have this running smoothly by the end of our Q1 – 1 November 2021.	Yes, although we do not micromanage or engage in witch hunts.	Yes, however, this is done on a selective audit basis, as opposed to routinely on all projects.
Yes, we review our projects as they complete, and this feeds back into our fee bids. Most recently we have reviewed our risk share proposal with clients in light of changing requirements within bid consortiums. The industry trend for more information earlier in the process – BIM etc. – means we have had to reduce our risk share offer on Stages 1–3 – pre financial close.	Not so much. We will refer more to the financial performance and fee levels. We do use historic costs to develop our own fee scales.	Yes.

Table continues

	Vagdia and Holmes Chartered Architects	Gbolade Design Studio	The Bazeley Partnership Chartered Architects
How far ahead do you programme your resources?	We try to programme three months in advance, although the director's cash flow forecast is currently running five months ahead of the current date.	3 months.	It varies according to project size and the extent or scope of service. So, for smaller projects, where we are engaged for Stages 0/1 to 4, three months; but for larger projects, across all stages, a minimum of six months, which is reviewed and extended on a monthly basis so that we are 'blocking out time' and resource as required.
How frequently do you update your office programme?	This is done on a weekly basis, minimum.	On a weekly basis.	Weekly. Leaving it for much longer starts to cause problems!

Willmore Iles Architects Ltd	Buttress Architects	rg+p
We resource as far ahead as we are able against agreed fees. For large projects this can be 12–18 months ahead.	We try to look 3 months ahead, but even that is a work of fiction. A month is more realistic.	As far ahead as possible. Some projects with well-defined programmes, especially those with long-term build plans, will have resource plans that run for longer periods. Routinely, we focus on the upcoming three-month period.
All information referred to above is reviewed monthly at the SLT meeting and in between as required. The Deltek updates are done as soon as anything changes – so each project is a 'live' document.	We meet to review every 2 weeks and expect resources to be updated in advance of that. We expect our project managers to maintain their CMap project data sets.	It is a live document/system, with changes being made as and when they are needed. Depending on the project, this could be daily, weekly or monthly. This is generally reviewed on a weekly basis.

Appendix B

Professional indemnity insurance: writing to report an issue

When an issue occurs that suggests to you there may be a problem brewing, or if you receive an email which is a borderline allegation against you for something you have done – or haven't done but should have – you need to bring the matter to the attention of your professional indemnity insurance (PII) broker. Your policy will usually oblige you to bring to your insurer's attention any situation that might lead to a claim. Set out the situation clearly, and provide the information your broker will need to assess the impact if an allegation were to follow. If you receive an actual allegation, the same procedure applies.

Your communication to your broker should include relevant details about the project, such as your client appointment, the value of the work, the scope of your services and the fee you have charged. State what you think is the issue, what you think you could have done better and what would be the result of the event occurring (if it hasn't already), and give an assessment of the cost to fix it. Also include your suggested response to your client, for your broker to assess *before* you send it.

The following is a starter layout that might help you to assemble your first contact about a circumstance with your broker. The headings might help you to include all the information your broker will need. It will take time to prepare your information, but when you receive an email or letter from your client notifying you of an issue, it has to be dealt with straight away.

Dear *[broker's name]*

PROJECT NAME AND ADDRESS

CLIENT NAME

I am writing to advise you of a circumstance which might lead to a claim in relation to the above property: *[describe property, e.g. new build, two storeys, residential etc.]*.

The issue

Today *[date]* we received the attached correspondence* from *[sender]* setting out their concerns over the following:

List the concerns raised.

**Alternatively, it may have been a comment made or a phone call – describe what it was that makes you think there could potentially be a claim.*

The contract

Our Agreement / appointment of *[date]* is attached. It describes the services we agreed to provide as follows:

Describe the scope of services.

The terms of our Agreement state our liability as *[describe liability period – e.g. 6 years]*.

The background

Describe here the relevant facts of the matter – for example, dates of any permissions obtained, dates of instructions to make a change to the scope of services, etc.

Include details of the building contract if works are on site, with dates of commencement, practical completion etc.

Include details of other consultants and information they may have provided and when.

List out anything pertinent to the allegation or potential allegation, with dates of when they happened, such as site inspections or significant correspondence.

It can sometimes help to set out the above in a timeline – only include relevant information.

My observations

Use this section to comment on your understanding of the issue raised. If there are claims of defective work, for instance, examine your records/photos/meeting notes and give your views on the quality or otherwise of the defect. Be honest and highlight what, with hindsight, you might have been able to observe at the time, or if there is a mistake in the drawings/annotations/specification, bring it to your broker's attention here. Don't be afraid to go into detail about the technicalities in this section – this is your opportunity to demonstrate your expertise about the claim.

Possible remedy

Here, describe the remedial work likely to be required to make good what is at fault. Consider the processes involved, such as high-level access, dismantling completed work, relocation of occupants – whatever will be required to put right the problem. If you can assess the costs of the potential building works, include your estimate here.

Proposed response

Your broker will need time to assess the implications of the above, and the information might need to be sent on to your insurer for them to make a comment. You are obliged to respond to any complaint against you in a reasonable time. The Architects Code states this should be within 10 days.

> *10.2 Complaints should be handled courteously and promptly at every stage, and as far as practicable in accordance with the following time scales:*
>
> *a) an acknowledgement within 10 working days from the receipt of a complaint; and*
>
> *b) a response addressing the issues raised in the initial letter of complaint within 30 working days from its receipt.*[1]

1 ARB. *The Architects Code: Standards of Professional Conduct and Practice* (London: ARB, 2017). Available at: https://arb.org.uk/wp-content/uploads/2016/05/Architects-Code-2017.pdf [accessed 1 February 2022].

In order to ensure you are not held up in making a response, prepare a holding email/letter to send to your client, or whoever made the initial complaint, and set it out for your broker to comment on.

I have drafted an initial holding response below which I should like to send promptly:

They may be able to approve it promptly or, even if they have to send it to your insurer to approve (which is not uncommon), you will at least be able to request a quick reply to allow you to send it.

Your holding email needs to be brief and uncomplicated, such as:

> Dear ________, Thank you for your email of *[date]*. We have noted your comments and will be in touch in due course.

or

> Dear ________, Thank you for your letter of *[date]* which we received on *[date]* bringing to our attention your concerns. We aim to write to you again with our response by *[date]*.

It must not prejudice you in any way, nor refer to the fact you have involved your insurer.

I will advise of any further developments as they occur, in the meantime I can confirm that I have not yet sent my draft response above pending comments from you and the insurer.

I look forward to hearing from you.

Yours *etc.*

Appendix C

Agile working policy

Example agile working policy (courtesy of PLACE architects)

Agile Working

The practice has responded to the changing way people are working. Introducing agile working gives you choices within prescribed guidelines to improve your work–life balance.

It should empower you to choose the way you work, which in turn will deliver better results all round by motivating you to do a better job because you know you can balance work around your personal life, preferences and circumstances.

It reinforces how the practice values people by creating a more inclusive culture, promoting diversity and supporting those with commitments outside work. It also focuses on outputs and delivery rather than clock watching.

This has to work for everybody within the team and I hope that we can establish ways of working to suit all of us.

This policy sets out the options the practice has available.

1. Core working hours:

   1.1 This option presents you with an opportunity to choose when to start and end your working day provided you work certain 'core hours'.

   1.2 The designated period of the day when you must be working will normally be 09:30 to 16:00.

   1.3 You will make up the difference in your contractual hours – these are the hours you have agreed to work in your contract.

1.4 This type of arrangement could be helpful if you wish to avoid busy traffic periods, or with other commitments outside work such as the school run, club memberships, community groups etc.

1.5 This would be an informal agreement so there would be no change to your contract, but it will be important to agree the hours you will work. If the arrangement was going to be over a prolonged period, a formal agreement may be needed.

2. Compressed working hours:

2.1 This gives you the option to work your normal contractual hours over a shorter period rather than a normal five-day pattern, say.

2.2 You could work full-time over extended hours on four days and have a non-working day or another arrangement such as two half non-working days per week can be considered.

2.3 The most common pattern may end up as a four-day week or a nine-day fortnight.

2.4 In order to allow others in the team to better manage workload and programme, this type of arrangement would normally be fixed to permit better predictability.

3. Staggered hours:

3.1 This gives you the option to benefit from different start, finish and break times from the normal office routine.

3.2 It means you can plan your work pattern to suit your out-of-work commitments, such as going swimming mid-morning.

3.3 The office could start to benefit from offering a service over extended hours if an early/late shift pattern was adopted.

3.4 As above, this would normally need to be fixed to allow others in the team to know when to expect you to be in and when to expect you to be out.

4. Planning family leave:

4.1 It is important to be able to balance your career with family life.

4.2 If you qualify for maternity, paternity, parental, shared parental or carer leave, we can review your requirements and agree a planned period leave.

5. Sabbaticals:

5.1 This is a period of time over and above normal annual leave – away from work.

5.2 It could provide you with the opportunity to study, travel, join a volunteer programme or meet family-related obligations.

5.3 A sabbatical would be unpaid and can last 3 to 6 months.

5.4 These would have to be reviewed on a case-by-case basis and take into account how your work and responsibilities would be covered whilst you were away.

5.5 They may take some preparation, perhaps with a lead-in period, but it is important to know you have not left it too late (in life) to do what you once planned to do.

6. Return to work programme:

   6.1 When you return to work after maternity/paternity leave, long-term sickness or a sabbatical, we will support you in your return to work depending on your individual circumstances.

   6.2 This could include a combination of 'keep-in-touch' days during your time off, staggered starts, short-term working for an interim period and so on.

   6.3 It is important to ensure your return to work is timely and structured to get you back to work at the earliest opportunity.

7. Phased retirement:

   7.1 Now there is no Government default retirement age, you can choose when you want to retire.

   7.2 You may decide you no longer wish to work regular hours so you can request to reduce your hours or days as part of your transition towards retirement.

Agile working is a behavioural change and there may be some concerns about its impact generally, or how it will affect meeting operational or client requirements, your own measure of performance or how other peoples' flexible working may impact on you.

According to a report by the Chartered Institute of Personnel and Development, the top three benefits of flexible working most frequently cited by employees are:

1. it enables better work–life balance
2. it helps reduce the amount of stress/pressure employees feel under
3. it has been a factor in employees staying with their current employer.

Moving to agile working is a natural change, one suited to today's working environment and it should bring benefits such as more predictability of when staff are around, better punctuality, as well as promoting the practice as a progressive, people orientated company.

When you have considered the options on offer and you have thought about why you think you could benefit from an agile working arrangement, please arrange to talk to the Office Manager. Some notes for your discussion would be useful, such as how you think any new arrangement would benefit you and the business, what the rest of the team might have already said to you about any revised working pattern. Also, if you have any concerns or questions or a suggestion for a trial period to see if it works.

INDEX

Note: page numbers in bold refer to tables.